GROWING
SELF-SUFFICIENCY

SALLY NEX

GROWING SELF-SUFFICIENCY

REALIZE YOUR DREAM AND ENJOY PRODUCING
YOUR OWN FRUIT, VEGETABLES, EGGS AND MEAT

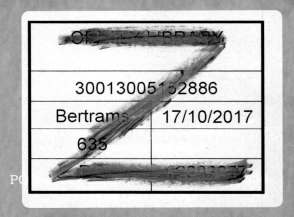

First published in 2017, in England

Sally Nex has asserted her moral rights under the Copyright, Designs and Patents Act 1988.

Front cover image © 2017 Naomi Schillinger

All interior photographs are by the author, with the exception of the following. Pages 2-3, 8, 15, 18, 34, 50, 68, 142, 144 (bottom), 147, 156, 168, 184, 198: Naomi Schillinger. Pages 78, 80: Shutterstock.com. Pages 132, 133: Brighton & Hove Food Partnership. Page 138: Su Johnston.

The publisher has endeavoured to identify all copyright holders, but will be glad to correct in future editions any omissions brought to its notice.

Design by Jayne Jones

ISBN: 978-0-85784-317-3 (paperback)
ISBN: 978-0-85784-318-0 (EPUB)
ISBN: 978-0-85784-319-7 (PDF)
Also available on Kindle

Disclaimer: the advice herein is believed to be correct at the time of printing, but the author and publisher accept no liability for actions inspired by this book.

10 9 8 7 6 5 4 3 2 1

FSC
www.fsc.org

MIX
Paper from
responsible sources
FSC® C016779

Contents

To Jonathan, Ellie and Ruby
with endless love and thanks for being the guinea pigs

Acknowledgements

This has been a lifetime's journey, so I'd have to write another book to give due credit to everyone who has helped me along the way: gardeners are an amazingly helpful and generous bunch, and I am constantly humbled by how willing everyone has been to share their knowledge, experience, wisdom and time.

Particular thanks must go to the following people and organizations. Naomi Schillinger, for her cheerful generosity and patience in the face of recalcitrant chickens; Angela Sharp, for her limoncello recipe; Abigail Norton; Zoe Lynch; Claire Pearce; Andrea and Clive Woods; Michelle Wallbridge; Starchild in Glastonbury, for their permission to take photos in their magical shop; the Royal Horticultural Society, whose flower shows have provided years of inspiration; the National Trust; River Cottage, Devon; Sarah Garland, my oracle on all things herbal; Surrey Docks Farm, London; the Brighton & Hove Food Partnership; the allotment holders of South Petherton; Su Johnston and all at Grace & Flavour Community Garden; and Combe St Nicholas Primary School.

I'd also like to thank the infinitely patient and good-humoured team at Green Books. Niall, Alethea, Jayne, Sheila and Lindsey: you all deserve a medal.

Foreword

I remember well taking home from my allotment my first crops, for my mother to cook; then the enjoyment of eating fresh food that I had grown myself, knowing exactly what had happened to it and what had been put on it. I was eleven years old. That thrill remains with me to this day, and it is clear from the enthusiasm that leaps from these pages that Sally gains the same satisfaction from being as self-sufficient as possible.

Sally writes from a practical point of view, not only showing the novice how to make a start but also including plenty to make the more seasoned gardener challenge conventional ways of producing food. She shows how even without a garden you can go a long way to providing for yourself from window boxes and containers.

Written in an easy-to-follow manner and full of handy tips, this book should inspire and reassure first-timers who may be experiencing problems. Advice born of hard-earned experience encourages all to have a go and to think about where their food, drink and medicines come from. For the experienced reader who is really getting to grips with this way of living, there are interesting ideas, recipes and suggestions for crops, products and growing methods.

Sally questions the loss of seasonality in modern eating habits, highlighting the value of good storage methods to ensure continuity of supply throughout the year. She explains how to keep your crops going by saving your own seed and propagating your own plants.

For some time now, many people have been turning away from the rush and bustle of modern life. They are aware of what has gone into the food we obtain from many supermarkets. They are more inquisitive, searching and discerning, and wish to return to food that is truly fresh, without contamination in any sense. This book provides many of the answers to questions that are being raised, and will inspire you to embrace a lifestyle that is achievable in today's world. Happy growing to you all.

Christine Walkden

Introduction

I didn't intend for this to happen. I used to grow delphiniums, roses and clipped box hedges. I worried about tulip combinations (well, I still do that a bit). I started growing a few veg just for a laugh, really – just to see if I could. I realized, a few mouthfuls too late, how easy it can be to get hooked beyond salvation after eating a handful of fresh broad beans from my first experimental veg bed: a decidedly bijou sliver of earth spared, rather grudgingly, from my already small and overstuffed London garden.

Those half-dozen broad bean plants were the start of everything. It wasn't long before I had French beans up the fences; herbs shoehorned into a patio where you fought the tomatoes and salads for leg room before you could sit down. I yearned for the kind of space where I could grow whole meals from the garden – enough room to pick and eat everything my family needed for the kitchen, fresh and as nature intended it to be.

Taking control of your own food is one of the easiest ways to tread lighter on the earth: as easy, in fact, as planting a seed. At a stroke, armed with nothing more high-tech than a row of beans, you can step gracefully off the global merry-go-round of plastic packaging, food miles, waste, intensive agriculture, soil degradation, habitat loss, neonicotinoids and poisoning yourself and your family with the cocktail of chemicals poured daily on the 'fresh' food on supermarket shelves.

And best of all, it's not the all-or-nothing choice so many make it out to be. Self-sufficiency in at least some of our food is within reach of us all, wherever we live, whatever we do: no lifestyle change required. You don't have

One plant in a pot – and you're self-sufficient in rosemary.   A few roomy containers will provide all the salad you can eat.

to give up the day job and go live on a smallholding in the hills; nor is it compulsory to gut rabbits on the kitchen table (unless you really want to).

Plant a chilli pepper in a pot on your windowsill, and suddenly you can have fresh chillies all summer, and dried ones all winter too. Save some seed, and you've got chillies for as long as you want them. Rosemary is another one: you need just one plant, as it's evergreen, and long-lived, so you can pick it year-round pretty much indefinitely. It's perfectly happy in a pot too. You see – you don't even need a garden.

Or perhaps you want to wean yourself off your bagged salads habit (quite apart from the plastic packaging and food miles required to get them to the supermarket, the chemicals they've been drenched in to keep them fresh include powdered fruit acids and chlorine). Sow three containers, a month apart, with a baby-leaf seed mix and you've got your own totally organic, natural supply ready for the picking, 12 months of the year. You don't have to worry about what's happened to it before it reached your plate, and you've achieved a level – however modest – of proper self-sufficiency.

It is a bit addictive. Supplying your own needs through your own efforts seems to waken some deep, atavistic instinct that is hard to suppress again. Perhaps it's the caveman hard-wired into our genes – but all I can say is that growing your own food is deeply, deeply satisfying, and once you've taken the first step towards providing for yourself you'll just want to keep adding more to the list of things you can produce for yourself.

Achieving self-sufficiency in most of the fresh foods you eat is really a matter of good old-fashioned vegetable gardening. There is a subtly different mindset required, though: instead of growing a few beans for fun, to supplement your diet, you have to think in terms of supplying produce to keep you going year-round. That takes a more belt-and-braces approach. You spend a lot of time planning, and develop a slightly obsessive attention to detail. It is a little scary that I know the average number of cabbages my family eats in a year. But I need to, so I can grow that number – no more, or I'm wasting valuable growing space, and no fewer, or we go without cabbage.

Do it for long enough and you'll also notice a subtle change in the way you think about your food. It's not anything dramatic: just a shift in perception really. You start to tune in to the seasons: your eating habits guided not by recipe books or the discount shelf at the supermarket but by your garden.

Instead of grabbing a plastic-wrapped packet of haggard French beans from the shelves in midwinter, you wander down the garden path and see if the purple sprouting broccoli is ready yet (if not, there's always kale). Instead of picking out a recipe from a book and tracking down the ingredients it demands, you decide what you're going to cook when you know what's in your outdoor larder.

It's a kind of delayed gratification we're not used to these

If it's too early for purple sprouting broccoli, there's always kale.

Seasonal eating brings a new excitement to the daily diet.

days, but once you adjust you'll find it makes your day-to-day menu so much more interesting. I can't remember ever getting excited about my food before I started to grow my own, but nowadays my family has more food-related celebrations than we even knew were possible. The arrival of the first asparagus spears is a red-letter day of much anticipation, we celebrate the first blackcurrants with a monster cheesecake, and we invite friends over for a barbecue to savour the first of that year's fresh lamb.

So trust yourself. Just try out one, or more, of the adventures into self-sufficiency I outline in this book, with no other changes to your daily life, and you will discover your own ability to provide for yourself. If nothing else, it gets you really thinking, seriously, about where your food comes from and how it's produced – and it'll give you a sense of pride like you've never felt before.

HOW TO USE THIS BOOK

You may want to go all out for as much self-sufficiency as you can muster from the start, or perhaps you just want to dip a toe in, to see how you get on. Here you'll find chapters designed for every level of enthusiasm. Perhaps you want to start by growing just the easiest foods: things like chard, salads, chillies and kale, which you can have about the place all year round, with minimum effort. Or maybe you're already growing a few veg and want to provide a wider range of fresh food for yourself. Part One of this book guides you through all the techniques you need for a respect-able level of self-sufficiency, including successional sowing, seasonal eating and expanding the range of what you grow: in fact, generally getting your head around the regular routine of sowing and harvesting required to provide a constant supply of food for you and your family. If you're not too confident in your gardening abilities, you'll find a helpful guide to the veg-growing basics in Chapter 6, at the end of Part One.

If you're getting hooked on this self-sufficiency kick (and you will), I'll tell you how to find yourself some more land and get seriously ambitious. In Part Two you'll find ways of supplying other areas of your life from your garden, from the drinks in your cupboard to the medicines on your shelves. And in the last chapter I look at going all the way and producing your own eggs and meat, even if you don't have a smallholding to call your own. You should be able to increase your level of self-sufficiency at your own speed and to suit your own taste, until you're sitting down to a meal you've completely grown yourself.

Start with growing the easy stuff – and go as far as you want to.

Make the step up from a garden to an allotment, and you'll have room to grow all the fresh food you need for a family of four.

A lot of the time I can only touch on the possibilities – this book would be the size of an encyclopedia if I went into every detail about each aspect of self-sufficiency covered here! Producing your own food is an absorbing and lifelong journey of discovery, and you find out more every day. So I've put together some of my favourite sources of information, advice and in-depth expertise in the Resources section at the end, so you can explore further and follow your own road in whichever direction it takes you.

HOW MUCH SPACE DO YOU NEED?

Answer: not as much as you'd think. In fact, for some types of fruit and veg all you need is three roomy containers. This is how I supply my family with salads every year: I explain how in Chapter 2. A clever choice of veg helps too – in Chapter 1 you'll find out how to use what space you have to the max, growing the veg whose default option is year-round supply. Squeeze in some easy-care herbs and even fruit (turn to Chapter 4) and you'll always have something to pick.

For full year-round self-sufficiency in a wide range of fruit, veg and herbs, though, including extras like a patch of medicinal and cosmetic herbs, you're aiming at a plot roughly the size of a UK allotment. That's a roomy garden, measuring around 21m x 10.5m (70' x 35'). Providing your own meat and eggs requires more serious space – though again, not as much as you might expect. You'll find the recommended land requirements for livestock species in Chapter 13: it varies from a few square feet (for bees) to 2-3 acres (for sheep).

So you don't need a smallholding. In fact, you don't even need any land of your own. All the land I produce my food on, bar the actual garden, is borrowed. Just keep your eyes open, put the word out, put an ad in the back of your local paper, post on Facebook . . . whatever it takes to winkle out the patches of unloved land near you. You'd be amazed what's out there: you just need to go and find it.

A BIT ABOUT ME

My own self-sufficiency journey has taken me from a pea plant called Cedric on the windowsill of my childhood bedroom (I know, I know – but I still remember the taste of those peas) via a pocket-handkerchief of London clay to an allotment in suburbia.

Now it's all got well out of hand, and somewhere along the way I seem to have acquired a small flock of sheep, a motley gaggle of chickens and a wild and rather woolly chunk of wind-swept hillside in Somerset, in the south-west of England. I still manage to work full-time and referee a couple of teenagers, so my life hasn't changed that much; it's just got a bit busier.

Little by little I've taken responsibility for what I and my family consume, and along the way discovered how different it is to eat food perfectly fresh, untainted by chemicals and just as nature intended – wonky shapes, holey leaves, fabulous swoon-inducing flavour and all. You end up wanting to expand what you grow just so you don't have to eat the tasteless stuff from the store any more. I'm not there yet, wherever 'there' is, and I probably never will be: self-sufficiency isn't a goal but a journey; a process; a way of life. And I love every minute of it.

From curiously named windowsill plants to self-sufficiency in food: it's been quite a ride.

Part One
SOWING THE SEED

Kale is a real trooper, keeping you in year-round cabbagey leaves for minimum effort.

Chapter One
GROW THE EASY HITS

"A few key vegetables provide the backbone of your food-growing, all year round."

There are some veg that are so easy to grow that it's a mystery to me why they're still on the shelves (and usually at extortionate prices too). These are the self-sufficiency easy hits: the ones you can start growing right now, whether you garden on a windowsill or an allotment.

The best easy hits are with you all year round – the veg-growing equivalent of store-cupboard staples. Even windowsill growers need never be without fresh chillies, coriander (cilantro) and crisp baby-leaf salad to enjoy every day of the year. With a few square feet of outdoor garden, you can add succulent leafy chard and beefy kale as your veg for all seasons. That's five things crossed off the grocery list already!

This chapter gives you the low-down on the key vegetables you can rely on as the backbone of your food-growing. I've given quantities for a typical family of four, but of course if you're growing for smaller or larger numbers, scale up or down accordingly. All these easy veg are incredibly productive, and the 'top five' are always there when you need something to pick – winter or summer. Have these growing somewhere in your garden all the time, and you won't go far wrong.

With a bit of planning, you can have all the easy hits somewhere in the plot all year round.

Baby-leaf salads: a doddle to grow and a must-have for easy self-sufficiency.

YEAR-ROUND PRODUCE

There are two important things to get right if you want to supply a vegetable year-round. The first is quantity: always grow more than you think you'll need. Growing extras means you're insured against the cat deciding to sunbathe in your salad-filled window boxes or the entire local slug population descending on your patch of chard seedlings. It also means you can really raid your supplies from time to time, say if you have friends round.

The second nut to crack is your winter supplies. Some leafy veg, like kale and chard (especially the white-stemmed varieties of chard), are resilient enough to keep doggedly growing whether it's T-shirt weather or finger-numbing frost outside. All you need to do is remember to sow your overwintering crop before the end of the summer. Pop a cloche (row cover) over leafy veg through really foul weather, though: they'll survive snow, gales and lashing rain, but left unprotected the leaves are often unappetizingly shredded.

Failing year-round hardiness, crops which store well make good staples. Dried chilli peppers, for example, add the same spiciness and flavour to a dish as fresh ones, and keep forever, so you can enjoy that mouth-blistering heat all year round. And there's a whole range of other veg that are really good keepers, expanding your self-sufficiency repertoire to include almost-year-round staples. In particular, long-keeping winter squash like the 'Hubbard' varieties stay as fresh as the day you pick them for 6 months or more. Well-dried shallots store even better than onions, and if you pack root vegetables such as beetroot and turnips into boxes of damp sand, they'll stay in a state of suspended animation, plump and ready to eat, for up to 3 months after you've pulled them.

THE TOP FIVE EASY HITS

These are the five veg I wouldn't be without. They're the ones I know I can rely on to keep putting up more leaves, flowers and fruit year-round, even while my attention is elsewhere for a while. All can be grown wherever you live: you can even enjoy kale year-round from a window box if you sow it densely and pick it as young baby leaves. Start with easy-peasy salads and build up to chillies and coriander, then add in a selection from the other veg listed at the end of this chapter (which are almost year-round), and you can guarantee something home-grown on the plate every single day.

These days, your baby-leaf salad might include lemony sorrel, peppery mizuna or annual herbs.

Easy hit no. 1: Baby-leaf salads

I don't know what my family would do without salads. It's our default solution for greenery, no matter what we're eating: pasta, steaks, pie and chips, fried chicken . . . just add a handful of mixed baby salad leaves and a splash of French dressing, and you give any meal some style.

Salads weren't always this popular. Conventional salads (floppy lettuce leaves, sliced tomatoes and cucumbers arranged in concentric circles – remember those?) are now firmly consigned to the 1980s, along with big hair, ra-ra skirts and shoulder pads. In the age of ready-to-eat bagged salad, your baby-leaf salad these days is just as likely to include red-veined lemony sorrel, a peppery punch of mizuna or annual herbs such as chervil or coriander.

You can sow salads ready-mixed too. And they'll grow anywhere – in tin cans stapled to a wall; in troughs or wine crates. And, of course, in the ground, though it's party time

Just a handful of mixed salad leaves will add zest and style to any meal.

for slugs if you sow them direct. Instead, start mixed salads in a seed tray, then break up the seedlings into chunks to plant out at a wider spacing. Or just sow one pinch to a cell in module trays, to pop out and plant as little clumps to grow on.

Grow summer salads during the warmer months, then, in late summer, switch to hardier winter mixes and grow them under cover. I pack the borders of my greenhouse with pre-sown salads the moment I've pulled out the tomatoes: if I've timed the sowing right, I've got sturdy youngsters almost at picking size to see me right through winter.

Red-veined sorrel makes an unusual lemony salad leaf.

Growing guide

Season: Year-round.

Varieties: Opt for an easy life and buy pre-blended seed mixes such as 'Misticanza', which is a good summer mix of light, fresh flavours – or mix your own. A selection of aromatic herbs (coriander, for example) adds interest to summer lettuces like 'Salad Bowl'; ring the changes with pea shoots and baby-leaf chard or 'Red Russian' kale (see pages 23-6). Switch to a winter mix in colder weather: baby kale leaves, hardy orientals like mizuna, and spicy mustards blend well with corn salad and winter lettuces such as 'Merveille des Quatre Saisons' and 'Black Seeded Simpson'.

How much to grow:

On windowsills and patios: Three window boxes or troughs on the go provides generous pickings.

In the garden: A short 1.2m (4') row sown each month will keep you well supplied.

How to sow: From early spring onwards, sow quite thickly on to the surface of a container of compost and cover lightly with more compost.

Care: Salads prefer a slightly shady spot – too much heat and they'll bolt for the sky. Keep them damp, and feed occasionally with a capful of general-purpose liquid fertilizer such as seaweed in the watering can (or make your own fertilizer – see Chapter 12, page 209).

Pests and diseases: Slugs are your main enemy: protect crops with wildlife-friendly slug pellets, 'slug pubs' and night patrols (see also Chapter 6). Botrytis (grey mould)

also attacks if you overwater your salads, so keep them damp but not dripping wet.
Harvesting: Once your salad leaves are about 10cm (4") high, snip them away with scissors, leaving about 2cm (1") in the ground to re-sprout. You should get two or three harvests from each sowing.

Easy hit no. 2: Chard

Spinach is a bit of a love-it-or-hate-it vegetable. Those who love it swear by its fine flavours and strength-building nutritional value (I thought this was a myth made up by the people who draw Popeye cartoons, but it turns out to be true – mind you, you have to chow through a whole kilo of spinach every day to get much effect). For those who don't like it, it's just plain slimy. Plus it's fiendishly difficult to grow well, as it bolts (runs to flower) the moment you turn your back. So forget spinach: grow chard instead.

Chard, and its close relation perpetual spinach (also known as leaf beet), is often seen as the poor relation to spinach, but I think it's vastly superior. It keeps its crunch when you cook it, and comes with a side order of crisply succulent midrib – a bit like celery – in pretty shades of red, yellow, green and orange.

Chard is also ridiculously easy to grow. It's drought-tolerant, so fine for containers, and hardy, especially the white-stemmed Swiss chard, which soldiers on through the bitterest winter. Once you're into the rhythm of twice-yearly sowings (one in spring, one in the middle of summer), you'll have spinachy greens for every day of the year.

Chard makes an easy-option spinach substitute – with a side order of crunchy, succulent midrib.

If all you have is a window box, try growing chard as a punchily flavoured baby-leaf salad ingredient. In a larger container or in the open garden, you can let the plants reach full size and pick them leaf by leaf. They'll keep good-naturedly re-growing, over and over again, for months.

Growing guide

Season: Year-round.

Varieties: Swiss chard (with white stems) is the hardiest, especially the monster-sized 'Fordhook Giant'. If you're growing for looks, choose 'Ruby Chard', with its wine-red stems which glow like stained glass when the sun catches them.

How much to grow:

On windowsills and patios: Chard grows well in troughs and large pots: sow thickly to grow as baby leaves, or allow four or five plants to mature per trough or roomy container.

In the garden: Plant at 35cm (14") spacings, and keep six or seven plants on the go to provide spinachy leaves all year.

How to sow: Start in early spring, sowing in modules under cover. Later, sow straight into the ground outside. For baby leaves, simply scatter seed fairly thickly across a pot of compost and cover lightly with more compost. Remember to make a second sowing in the middle of summer to take over cropping through autumn and winter.

Care: Chard is one of the easiest crops you'll ever grow. In the open garden it grows in most soils and in sun or shade, and you shouldn't need to water it at all except in the driest of droughts. Winter crops should survive the harshest weather, though a cloche over the top helps prevent leaves shredding into unappetizing tatters.

Pests and diseases: Chard is wonderfully pest-free, and little seems to bother it except slugs, which attack seedlings (if you have problems, raise them under cover and transplant them outside when bigger).

Harvesting: For baby leaves, harvest at 10cm (4") tall, snipping them away 2cm (1") above compost level, and they'll re-grow a few times more. For full-sized plants, pick leaf by leaf, from the outside in, so the plant stays productive for as long as possible. Slice the green leaves off the stems to cook like spinach, while the broad midribs make very good celery substitutes in cooking. Both parts can be frozen successfully.

Easy hit no. 3: Kale

Kale was labelled with the 'superfood' badge shortly after it was 'discovered', and graduated from cattle feed to gourmet delicacy practically overnight. And with good reason: more iron than beef; more calcium than milk; over half your daily allowance of vitamin C in a mere 100g (4oz) – it should be available on prescription.

It's also a great house guest in the garden. Unusually, for a brassica, it doesn't need much special treatment to speak of. It doesn't even seem to notice, let alone complain, when it gets cold; it's extremely generous; and it's never boring, as it comes in enough varieties to keep you interested for years.

Grow baby-leaf kale like salads, sown thickly into window boxes or troughs year-round. If you've got room for full-sized plants, you're spoilt for choice in the range of varieties (see

Kale comes in a pick-and-mix range of shapes, sizes and colours (this is the red, frilly-leaved 'Redbor').

below) – try a new variety each year, or mix 'n' match for multiple choice through the season. There are purple curly kales too, and asparagus kale, which sends up tender, delicately flavoured flower spears in late spring to eat like broccoli. Not bad for cattle food!

Growing guide

Season: Year-round.
Varieties: Choose 'Red Russian' for salads (like a smoky purple lettuce with attitude). For winter growing, either the frizzy green 'Dwarf Green Curled' (my personal favourite) or 'Redbor' (burgundy, darkening in frost). The exotically dark and rumpled 'Black Tuscan', also known as 'Cavolo Nero', is handsome, with puckered, strappy leaves, but it's slightly less hardy.

How much to grow:
On windowsills and patios: Kale *can* grow in containers – especially smaller varieties like 'Red Russian' – but this works best if it's grown for picking very young, as baby leaves. Sow one trough or roomy container every month for a continuous supply.
In the garden: Six or seven full-grown plants allow regular picking.
How to sow: Sow baby-leaf kale quite thickly on to the surface of a container of compost and cover lightly. For mature plants, sow into 5cm (2") modules in spring (for summer picking) and early summer (for winter greens), as direct sowings tend to fall prey to slugs. Move seedlings into a cooler cold frame until they're ready to plant out.

Care: Kale is that rare thing, a virtually trouble-free brassica. Firm it in well when you plant it out, and stake taller varieties to prevent them toppling over in winter gales. And that's about it.

Pests and diseases: Again, compared with other brassicas, kale is amazingly easy-going. Birds like kale seedlings (so net plants while young), and caterpillars and mealybugs can be a nuisance, but growing under insect-proof mesh largely solves those problems.

Harvesting: The secret to enjoying your kale is to pick it young – so choose young leaves close to the crown, no more than 10cm (4") long, and snap them away leaf by leaf. The crown simply continues producing more to replace those it's lost, so it's not unusual to get 3 months of pickings from each plant. For salads, harvest as for other baby leaves (see page 23, top).

Easy hit no. 4: Chilli peppers

Fresh chillies are a luxury item in the shops, but all it takes is a few plants at home and you'll never need chilli powder again. Pick fruits as they ripen, then store your surplus to pep up your cooking till the next crop is ready. Dry the seeds and you've got your next batch of plants for free too.

It takes practice to grow chillies well, and you can make or break your chances with your choice of variety. All love warmth and sunshine, and some really sulk in low light and cold. Super-hot chillies such as the notoriously fiery 'Bhut Jolokia' are especially fussy.

Medium-hot chillies like 'Cayenne' or 'Jalapeno' are reasonably happy in cooler conditions, but for reliable self-sufficiency in chillies if you're growing in a temperate climate, track down the most cold-tolerant varieties (see below). Whichever variety you grow, let your chillies bake during the growing season. The hotter they are, the happier they'll be. Ideally, grow them in a greenhouse or on a sunny windowsill all season: plants kept outside may fruit, but nowhere near as prolifically as those indoors.

Chillies get hotter as they ripen, so you're missing out on half the flavour if you pick them while they're still green. Once they've coloured up nicely, pick all the fruit off and store for winter. Thin-skinned varieties like 'Cayenne' dry well, but if you're growing fleshier varieties, freeze them instead: you can remove the seeds if you like, but I just freeze them whole. When you need one, just pick it out of the bag and you'll find it will slice from frozen, with its flavour and heat just as good as when fresh.

Growing guide

Season: Year-round (fresh-picked in summer, and from store in winter).

Species and varieties: The annual chilli, *Capsicum annuum*, is the most widely grown: 'Prairie Fire' and 'Numex Twilight' are reliable choices for containers. But the chilli family is a large one, so have fun getting to know the less well-known varieties. The most cold-tolerant varieties are *C. pubescens*, also known as tree chillies,

A few chilli plants at home and you've got year-round heat for the kitchen.

including the super-generous 'Rocoto Red', with its lipstick-red, fiery-hot fruits; and *C. baccatum*. *Capsicum baccatum* 'Aji Amarillo' is orange, while 'Aji Limon' has a tangy citrusy flavour. Both 'Rocoto' and 'Aji' chillies tolerate mild frost, to about -2°C (28°F), and easily survive winter in a frost-free greenhouse. Both species grow to sizeable plants over time, though, so need plenty of room, but the payback is that they're more prolific the older they get.

How much to grow:

On windowsills and patios: Two or three chilli plants grown in 17.5cm (7") pots fit easily on a windowsill and provide as many chillies as you'll ever need.

In the garden: If you have a greenhouse, one large *Capsicum pubescens* or *C. baccatum* is all you need for a surfeit of chilli peppers. Otherwise, retreat to your windowsills: chillies are one of the few no-garden veg, and much prefer the warmer conditions indoors.

How to sow: Sow four or five seeds to a 10cm (4") pot in early spring and place in a heated propagator set to 20-25°C (68-77°F). Pinch out the top set of leaves once plants reach 10cm tall, to encourage them to grow bushy.

Care: Treat chillies a little mean to get the hottest peppers, watering only once the compost begins to dry out. Feed with a capful of high-potassium liquid feed in the watering can (ordinary tomato feed will do) once a fortnight, as soon as the plants begin to set flowers.

Pests and diseases: Lush, leafy chillies are adored by aphids, whitefly and red spider mite. Check regularly under leaves and on stems, and squash aphids on sight – or, if infestations get too bad, spray with insecticidal soap.

Harvesting and storing: Green chillies have not yet developed their full heat: the longer you wait, the hotter they get. Dry them, or freeze them whole (see page 26) – they keep exceptionally well, staying good for a year or sometimes more.

Decorative chillies

Dry chillies in a necklace or a traditional South American 'ristra' (rather like a bunch of grapes) and they'll look gorgeous hanging from a hook in the kitchen. Thread a needle and poke it through the fleshy part of the stem – at right angles for a necklace or at 45 degrees to make a ristra.

Easy hit no. 5: Coriander (cilantro)

OK, this one's cheating a bit. Leafy coriander isn't reliably year-round unless you can guarantee a frost-free winter, but this wonderfully useful herb comes two ways. We love to eat the spicy, fragrant leaves by the fistful torn

Even when coriander bolts it's good news – not long now till a second crop of spicy seeds for the kitchen.

Keep coriander cool and well watered to encourage lots of leafy growth.

into salads all summer (it turns a bowl of mixed lettuce into something really special), then I fill spice pots with the papery seeds for winter curries. Any seeds that I don't use for cooking, I save to re-sow next year.

I grow my coriander in window boxes, mainly because I've found it's the best way of getting the quantities I like without having to transplant any seedlings. If there's one thing coriander doesn't like, it's being fiddled about with, so sow it exactly where it's going to grow.

Generous troughs of leafy coriander are the original movable feast. An early sowing in the greenhouse gets shunted out on to the patio once the weather warms up, then I just sow troughs wherever I can find space for

them throughout the summer. Come autumn, I shift the last batches into a cool greenhouse or cold frame. In mild winters, without any really hard frosts, I'm often still picking it during spring.

Coriander does love to bolt, though, and once it sends up that flower spike it rapidly stops producing leaves. Since I grow mine in containers and I'm a little haphazard with the watering, I generally have some bolting coriander around somewhere too. For once, though, that's not a problem: in fact I've been known to encourage coriander to bolt if I'm getting short of seeds. Wait till the seedheads have dried to a papery brown, up-end them into paper bags, and you've got your winter supplies sorted.

Growing guide

Season: Year-round (fresh-picked from spring to autumn, then seeds through winter).

Varieties: 'Calypso' is said to be slower to bolt, and 'Confetti' has fine, feathery leaves – but there's not much to choose between them, so plain old coriander is as good as any.

How much to grow:

On windowsills and patios: Three or four troughs on the go all year round is enough to provide generous pickings.

In the garden: Depending on how much you use, a 1.2m (4') row re-sown regularly through the season keeps the supplies well topped up.

How to sow: Sow quite thickly on to the surface of a container of compost. Cover thinly with more compost, water and leave: never try to transplant coriander, or it will bolt straight away. Sow outside in summer, or in a cool greenhouse or cold frame in autumn.

Care: Choose your best and brightest spot for coriander, as it sulks petulantly in anything less than 100-per-cent sunshine. Water daily to keep the compost consistently moist: as soon as coriander is too dry, too wet, too hot or too cold, it'll bolt. Add a capful of general-purpose liquid feed (such as seaweed) to the watering can once a week while plants are in full growth.

Pests and diseases: Slugs adore coriander seedlings, so check just-sown troughs every night, especially when it's raining, and despatch any molluscs you find straight away. But that's about all you need to worry about.

Harvesting and storing: Snip the leaves off about 2cm (1") above compost level, to let the crown re-grow (you'll get two or three harvests from each sowing). Once your coriander bolts, let it set seed and then, when the seedhead is papery and brown, tip it into a paper bag and shake it to release the large, easy-to-handle seeds.

ALMOST-ALL-YEAR-ROUND EASY HITS

You can add to your store-cupboard staples with easy-to-grow veg which may not quite be on your plate all year round, but very nearly. Most you can eke out well into winter too, with a little careful planning so you have plenty left over to squirrel away in store.

Grow them through summer to eat fresh, then dig up your last crop (make it a bumper one if it's to see you through till spring) and pack it into boxes, or dry and keep on a slatted shelf somewhere dry and cool. They'll go into suspended animation for up to 3 months, sometimes more if you're lucky, extending your harvest to 10 months out of 12.

Beetroot: Bombproof growing in the garden or in containers, it keeps well for about 3 months layered with damp sand in newspaper-lined crates (see Chapter 9, page 160).

Pick the leaves (sparingly) while your beetroot is growing, for an extra crop of earthily flavoursome greens.

Marrows: Eat small as courgettes (zucchini) through summer, then allow some to grow on into marrows, which will keep for up to 4 months if you cure them (see tip on page 32).

Shallots: Dry for a fortnight in the sun, and they'll stay scrumptious for 6 months or more.

Turnips: Store in damp sand like beetroot; they will keep for a similar length of time.

Winter squash: Most squash, including the ever-popular butternut types, store for around 3 to 4 months – though 'Hubbard' and 'Turk's Turban' often keep for up to a year: cure them first (see page 32).

Cure squash somewhere sunny, dry and warm before storing, and they'll last much longer.

PERENNIAL EASY HITS

The best returns of all in the self-sufficiency stakes are from veg that just come back year after year, reliable as clockwork, no extra effort required. Perennial vegetables are a small and select group – but they're the easiest self-sufficiency hits you'll ever make. Here are three of the best.

'Daubenton' kale

'Daubenton' is the most widely available variety of perennial kale, *Brassica oleracea* var. *ramosa*. It gives as much beefy, cabbagey baby kale leaves as you can eat, all year round. Grown from cuttings, as it doesn't set viable seed, it crops steadily for up to 5 years.

Babington's leek

Find this by its Latin name *Allium ampeloprasum* var. *babingtonii*. Plant the bulbs and they sprout slender garlicky 'leeks'. Cut them off

Curing marrows and squash

'Cure' marrows, squash and pumpkins before storing, letting the skins harden in sunshine for 2 weeks. Put bricks underneath them, so the air can circulate fully, and remove leaves if they're shading the fruit, to expose the skins to full sun. Once ready, they'll feel hard and sound hollow when knocked. If wet weather hits in the middle of curing, cut the fruits and move them indoors somewhere warm and dry, like a greenhouse, sunny conservatory or windowsill, to finish off (see Chapter 9 for more about storing).

Perennial 'Daubenton' kale crops steadily for about 5 years on the trot.

at ground level, and the bulbs just keep on sprouting: year-round, year-on-year leeks for none of the effort of annuals.

Walking onion

Also known as Egyptian onion or tree onion, walking onion's Latin name is *Allium cepa* Proliferum Group. You can use it in three ways: snip the greenery like spring onions, pickle the tiny bulbils at the top of the stem, then harvest some of the main bulbs for onions. As the bulbils ripen and grow heavier, they bend the stems down – and if they touch the ground, they will root and turn into new plants (hence 'walking').

Walking onion bulbils root where they touch ground.

For self-sufficiency in a whole range of vegetables, you just need seed, compost and some large containers.

Chapter Two
START A THREE-POT VEG PLOT

*"With a simple system of pots –
one just sown, one growing
along and one to pick – you
can grow a continuous supply
of veg in a perfect circle."*

You don't need to have a 20-acre smallholding to be self-sufficient in quite a respectable range of vegetables. You don't even need a garden. In fact, all you need to provide your supplies of a good variety of home-grown produce, year-round, is a handful of roomy pots. I haven't bothered buying bagged supermarket salads since I bought myself three big handsome clay pots and started using this method for baby-leaf salads. (Well, maybe once or twice, but only because I let the routine slip.)

Your potted veg plot isn't limited to salad leaves, either. Using the same principle, you can fill your plate with a dazzling range of scrumptious seasonal veg, including peas, beans, carrots, greens and herbs, from spring till autumn.

With container-grown veg you have more control over conditions and plenty of scope for creativity.

Growing in pots has some great advantages: in fact, I grow veg in containers every year just for the convenience, even though I have a garden as well. It gives you control over water and nutrients as well as temperature – pots are portable, so just bring them indoors if it's getting cold, and they'll keep on cropping. You avoid lots of the problems you would normally encounter in the open garden too. It's easier to defend container-grown veg against pests, and, because you're growing fast and changing the compost regularly between sowings, diseases don't ever get the chance to build up.

In this chapter I describe how to make the multi-pot system work for you. For simplicity, I describe the various options based on a three-pot set-up, since for most fast-maturing veg, three pots is plenty (assuming you're

feeding a 'typical' family of four – adjust accordingly to suit your own needs). For slower-maturing veg, you'll want to use a four-pot system to ensure a continuous supply of produce (some examples of four-pot plots are given on pages 43-4).

There are three main approaches to try. The one-crop plot majors on quantity, while the three-variety plot is a less time-consuming version of this, relying on clever use of different varieties to lengthen the cropping time. And then there's the mixed plot, with lots of different veg combined in mouthwatering ways. In the following pages I'll give you plenty of delicious pot 'recipes' to help you get started, but once you get the hang of it you can just adjust the flavours, colours and textures to fill your potted veg plot with your own personal favourites.

HOW IT'S DONE

A three-pot veg plot operates as a perfect circle. You always have one pot to pick, one or two growing along, and one you've only just sown. You can keep this going indefinitely – often right around the year. It's brilliantly flexible: have one three-pot veg plot and you'll feed yourself quite nicely. Two or three sets, and you'll feed a family. Grow mixed-veg potted plots, or specialize in herbs, or ratatouille ingredients, or pretty much anything your imagination comes up with.

The system works best with vegetables that grow rapidly; up and ready to harvest in a short space of time: things like salads, beetroot, peas and beans. Avoid really hefty plants: the big brassicas, like Brussels sprouts, purple sprouting broccoli and full-sized cabbages, are never going to be happy in a pot, and I've always found potatoes disappointing too. Such bulky, hungry plants just can't find enough room to spread their roots in the confines of a container.

Instead, look out for varieties marked 'dwarf' or 'patio', with smaller root systems that cope better with container-grown life. And stick to 'early' varieties, which mature sooner and are better suited to the high turnover rate of a three-pot system. It's great fun experimenting: the great beauty of your potted veg plot is that you can have it any way you want.

THE ONE-CROP-POT PLOT

The simplest three-pot plots work to give you a continuous supply of just one type of vegetable. Each potful of, say, salad or spinach or kale or beetroot is that bit further on than the next – so you get a continuous succession of crops reaching pickable size just as the previous one goes over (or you eat it all!).

Timing is of the essence. The length of time it takes your crop to get from sowing to harvest dictates the number of times you re-sow your pots. For quick croppers, it can be as often as once a month, but for plants that take 12 weeks to harvest you'll re-sow only three times a year.

You don't have to stick slavishly to the rules, though: snaffle a sneaky crop of beetroot when they're little crunchy 8-week-old table-tennis-balls, or keep your hands off till 10 weeks and pull them as a satisfying fistful. It

doesn't matter, as long as you do the same thing for all three pots, to avoid gaps in supply.

Cropping times also vary according to variety. A speedy and sweet early carrot like the 'Nantes' types is ready in 10 weeks, but if you're impatient you could go for the little round-rooted 'Parmex', pullable at 8 weeks. Again, as long as you sow the same variety in all three pots you'll have a constant stream to pick.

The weather can kick a gaping hole in your plans, however, so keep an eye on the sky and adjust your sowing schedule – and variety choice – accordingly. If it's chilly, sow faster-growing types in your first pot (such as 'Meteor' peas), but when you come to sow the

Chard adores containers, and those multicoloured stems look gorgeous too.

Most fast-growing veg, including beetroot and lettuce, grow well in a three-pot system.

Salad leaves are among the easiest three-pot crops to grow year-round.

second and the weather's warmed up, opt for a slightly slower choice (such as mangetout peas), to make sure your supply still matures at staggered intervals.

You can grow most of the leafy types of veg right around the year using this technique, especially if you have a cool greenhouse in which to overwinter them. Roots and fruits – carrots, peas, beans, turnips and so on – are summer-only crops, but you can still supply all you need from late spring through till the first frosts, and you can always add an extra pot or two at final sowing time, for a surplus harvest to freeze or store through winter.

And of course you can grow as many or as few three-pot veg plots as you like. I started off just growing baby-leaf salad, but it wasn't long before I added another three-pot combi, supplying aromatic leafy coriander to cut at

the same time (I adore coriander in salad). Then I just had to add a few bunches of spring onions in another pot system alongside. Once you start, it's kind of addictive. I just hope your patio is big enough!

Make your compost work for you

When re-sowing containers, there's no need to replace all the compost: just scrape out the top 5cm (2") and replace it with fresh. See also panel on pages 40-1 for info on nutrients in containers.

A wigwam of French beans in a roomy container gives you bowlfuls of crunchy beans to pick all summer.

Container-veg care

The larger your container is, the happier your plants will be, as they'll have more room to stretch out their roots. This is particularly important for large vegetables, such as calabrese, and for deep-rooted ones like carrots, which fork if they hit an obstacle. And the smaller your container, the more often you'll have to water it. By the same token, although you *can* cram veg into a container more closely than in the ground, due to the concentrated richness they're growing in, it does have its limits. Overcrowd your veg and you could end up with fungal diseases and weak, spindly, unproductive plants. So plant them fairly close, but give them room to grow: at least half the recommended garden planting distance is a good rule of thumb.

For vegetables growing in a three-pot system, the minimum pot size is 35cm (14") diameter and about 45cm (18") deep – though go bigger if you can (the larger the pot, the more food you get too). Troughs and Versailles planters often offer more room than the usual round pots: if you're handy with a hammer you can custom-build timber planters to fit your outdoor space.

Remember that growing in containers is a really intensive system, where every ounce of compost has to work hard to meet the needs of the hungry veg growing in it. So you need to really spoil your veg to keep them performing for you. Here's how.

Fill your pot with good-quality multipurpose compost. (When starting out, you'll probably find it easier to buy your compost in, but

Troughs make good roomy containers: use them like elongated veg patches, mixing kale, lettuce, spinach and beetroot in a gloriously yummy hotchpotch.

once you get hooked, try a home-made mix – see Chapter 12, page 212 for details. This is better for pots, as it's soil-based, so holds on to nutrients for longer.) Nutrient levels in non-soil-based composts start deteriorating after about 6 weeks, so at this point start feeding weekly with a general-purpose liquid feed such as seaweed or nettle tea, switching to high-potassium tomato feed or comfrey tea as your plants flower and fruit. You'll find recipes for home-made fertilizer 'teas' on page 209 of Chapter 12. You won't need to feed really fast-growing crops like baby-leaf salads, as they're in and out of the compost just too quickly. Just top them up with fresh compost each time you sow.

Keep the compost continuously damp, watering daily or twice daily in hot weather. An automatic dripper system helps save trips with the watering can. Test how moist the compost is by sticking your finger in as far as it will go: even if it's been raining and the surface is wet, it can be surprisingly dry down by the roots.

In general, a potted veg plot suffers from fewer pests than veg in the open ground, as long as plants don't go short of water or nutrients. But keep an eye out for aphids clustering on the underside of leaves (squash them on sight or spray with insecticidal soap), and protect plants against slugs (a particular danger for just-emerged seedlings).

One-crop-pot growing schedules

The following tables give an idea of the timings you'll need to follow for a continuous supply of your chosen crop. Week 1 of each schedule is the first week of early spring (which will vary depending on where you live: in most of the UK, for example, it's roughly the first week of March).

The trick with successful one-crop pots is to know how long your veg will take from sowing to maturity. That way you can work out how frequently to re-sow your next pot – and when you can expect to start picking.

For slower-growing veg – those that take more than 8 weeks till maturity – use a four-pot system to guarantee a constant supply.

Eight-week veg

These include salad leaves, rocket, baby-leaf chard, baby beetroot and 'Tokyo Cross' turnips.

Spring			
Week 1:	pot 1: sow (under cover)	pot 2: empty	pot 3: empty
Week 5:	pot 1: seedlings	pot 2: sow (outdoors)	pot 3: empty
Week 9:	pot 1: picking	pot 2: seedlings	pot 3: sow (outdoors)
Week 13:	pot 1: clear & re-sow (outdoors)	pot 2: picking	pot 3: seedlings
Summer			
Week 17:	pot 1: seedlings	pot 2: clear & re-sow	pot 3: picking
Week 21:	pot 1: picking	pot 2: seedlings	pot 3: clear & re-sow
Week 25:	pot 1: clear & re-sow	pot 2: picking	pot 3: seedlings
Autumn			
Week 29:	pot 1: seedlings	pot 2: clear & re-sow	pot 3: picking
Week 33:	pot 1: picking	pot 2: seedlings	pot 3: clear & re-sow (and sow extra pots for winter)*
(Now bring all pots into a cool greenhouse, porch or conservatory)			
Week 37:	pot 1: clear & re-sow (under cover)*	pot 2: picking	pot 3 plus extras: seedlings
Winter			
Week 41:	pot 1: seedlings	pot 2: clear	pot 3-plus: picking
Week 45:	pot 1: seedlings	pot 2: empty	pot 3-plus: picking
Week 49:	pot 1: seedlings	pot 2: empty	pot 3-plus: picking
Week 1 (Season 2):	pot 1: picking	pot 2: sow (under cover)	pot 3-plus: clear
. . . and start the cycle again.			

*For salads, use winter-hardy varieties.

Eight-to-ten-week veg

These include hearting lettuce, baby-leaf kale, peas, carrots, mid-season beetroot, kohlrabi and Chinese broccoli (also known as kailaan or stem broccoli).

Spring

Week 1: pot 1: sow (under cover)	pot 2: empty	pot 3: empty	pot 4: empty
Week 3: pot 1: seedlings	pot 2: sow (under cover)	pot 3: empty	pot 4: empty
Week 6: pot 1: seedlings	pot 2: seedlings	pot 3: sow (under cover)	pot 4: empty
Week 9: pot 1: picking	pot 2: seedlings	pot 3: seedlings	pot 4: sow (outdoors)
Week 12: pot 1: clear & re-sow (outdoors)	pot 2: picking	pot 3: seedlings	pot 4: seedlings

Summer

Week 15: pot 1: seedlings	pot 2: clear & re-sow (outdoors)	pot 3: picking	pot 4: seedlings
Week 18: pot 1: seedlings	pot 2: seedlings	pot 3: clear & re-sow (outdoors)	pot 4: picking
Week 21: pot 1: picking	pot 2: seedlings	pot 3: seedlings	pot 4: clear & re-sow
Week 24: pot 1: clear & re-sow	pot 2: picking	pot 3: seedlings	pot 4: seedlings
Week 27: pot 1: seedlings	pot 2: clear*	pot 3: picking	pot 4: seedlings

Autumn

Week 30: pot 1: seedlings	pot 2: empty	pot 3: clear	pot 4: picking
(Now bring all four pots into a cool greenhouse, porch or conservatory)			
Week 33: pot 1: picking	pot 2: empty	pot 3: empty	pot 4: clear & re-sow (under cover)*
Week 1 (Season 2): pot 1: clear & re-sow (under cover)	pot 2: empty	pot 3: empty	pot 4: picking
. . . and start the cycle again.			

*For lettuce, use winter-hardy varieties.

Ten-to-twelve-week veg

These include chard, full-grown spinach, dwarf French beans, maincrop carrots and mangetout peas. (NB: dwarf French beans are not hardy, so use these only for sowings from late spring to late summer.)

Spring

Week 1:	pot 1: sow (under cover)	pot 2: empty	pot 3: empty	pot 4: empty
Week 5:	pot 1: seedlings	pot 2: sow (under cover)	pot 3: empty	pot 4: empty
Week 9:	pot 1: seedlings	pot 2: seedlings	pot 3: sow (under cover)	pot 4: empty
Week 13:	pot 1: picking	pot 2: seedlings	pot 3: seedlings	pot 4: sow (outdoors)

Summer				
Week 17:	pot 1: clear & re-sow (outdoors)	pot 2: picking	pot 3: seedlings	pot 4: seedlings
Week 21:	pot 1: seedlings	pot 2: clear & re-sow (outdoors)	pot 3: picking	pot 4: seedlings
Week 25:	pot 1: seedlings	pot 2: seedlings	pot 3: clear*	pot 4: picking

Autumn				
Week 29:	pot 1: picking	pot 2: seedlings	pot 3: empty	pot 4: clear
(Now bring all four pots into a cool greenhouse, porch or conservatory)				
Week 33:	pot 1: clear & re-sow (under cover)*	pot 2: picking	pot 3: empty	pot 4: empty
Week 1 (Season 2):	pot 1: seedlings	pot 2: clear & re-sow (under cover)	pot 3: empty	pot 4: empty
. . . and start the cycle again.				

Use winter-hardy veg like chard.

THE THREE-VARIETY POTTED VEG PLOT

Don't want a load of empty pots hanging about while you wait to fill them? Then fill three of them at once. This way, you take advantage of the fact that different varieties of the same vegetable crop at different times. Sow one early-maturing, one mid-season-maturing and one late-season-maturing (maincrop) variety at the same time in spring. The early type will be ready to harvest first, a few weeks later you should have the mid-season one to pick, and at the end of the season you can enjoy the late variety. One sowing, three times the length of harvest, and you're self-sufficient for the whole of the season. And you can keep it going even longer by sowing a second batch of the early-maturing variety in late summer for picking in autumn, then you'll still be enjoying the harvest well into winter.

Some examples of crops and varieties you can try this with are given in the table below.

	Early-maturing	Mid-season-maturing	Late-maturing / maincrop
Calabrese	pot 1: 'Fiesta'	pot 2: 'Green Magic'	pot 3: 'Chevalier'
Carrots	pot 1: 'Paris Market'	pot 2: 'Nantes'	pot 3: 'Red Cored Chantenay'
Leeks	pot 1: 'King Richard'	pot 2: 'Musselburgh'	pot 3: 'Below Zero'
Peas	pot 1: 'Twinkle'	pot 2: 'Kelvedon Wonder'	pot 3: 'Cavalier'

Mix your own salads

I'm dreadfully fussy about my baby-leaf salads, and off-the-shelf seed blends are rarely just right. At least one of the leaves in the mix isn't what I'd have chosen – and I get particularly grumpy about hardy winter salad mixes, which always seem to overdo the peppery mustards, mizuna and chicories.

So I doctor my seed mixes. A pinch of extra herb seed added to the packet, or perhaps a teaspoon of gentler-flavoured winter lettuce seed to tone down those mustardy flavours, and you've got a bespoke mix that's uniquely, deliciously yours. Even better, develop your own salad mix: just measure a quarter- or half-teaspoon of seed of each of your favourite varieties into a bowl, stir and decant into a paper envelope ready to use.

To see you through the colder months, combine winter-hardy mustards with milder oriental veg like pak choi, plus winter leaves such as purslane.

Stick to varieties that mature at the same rate: it's no good mixing super-speedy rocket with slow-growing 'Red Russian' kale and expecting them to pop up at the same time. You're unlikely to get it perfect first time, either, so make notes, and adjust the mix each time until you've got the recipe just right.

Basic salad blends

Summer mix:
1 tsp 'Red Salad Bowl' lettuce
1 tsp 'Green Salad Bowl' lettuce
½ tsp 'Reddy' spinach
½ tsp coriander
½ tsp Greek cress

Winter mix:
1 tsp corn salad
1 tsp 'Black Seeded Simpson' lettuce
1 tsp 'Rouge d'Hiver' lettuce
½ tsp 'Red Frills' mustard
½ tsp mizuna

THE MIXED-POT VEG PLOT

It's all very well providing bucketloads of salad from my three containers, but I'm never content just to leave it at that. I start hankering after some peas, or a few beetroot, or maybe some kale. Trouble is, unless you have a patio the size of Times Square it's going to be a squeeze to provide a three-pot plot for every variety of vegetable you want to grow. That's where the mixed-pot veg plot comes in.

Mixed-veg pots combine two or three different crops to pick in the same container, each pot sown (just like the one-crop pots) a little later than the one before, to give you a continuous stream of veg to pick.

I think of my mixed-veg pots as bedding-plant combinations you can eat. Just as with bedding plants, you want 'one to thrill, one to fill and one to spill' – so I put something tall-ish in the middle (say, peas), surround it with a ring of leafy kale or chard, and find something low-growing – radishes, maybe, or salad leaves – for the outside. Since we're getting artistic, it's kind of fun choosing contrasting leaf colours, or different textures: feathery carrots against broad spinach leaves, for example. The end result can look every bit as good as your average pelargonium-and-petunia combo – and you can eat it.

Use your containers like mini veg plots and you can pick a huge variety of goodies from a tiny space.

Bush tomatoes make great centrepieces for a mixed container.

The system works best when you combine crops that have similar harvesting times. So keep one set of three pots for fast-growing 8-weekers (such as radishes, baby-leaf salads and 'Tokyo Cross' turnips), and group the 12-weekers (such as mature kale, chard and dwarf French beans) together in another. That way you can sow each group at the same, regular interval and keep picking right round the year.

You don't have to stick to exactly the same veg in each of the three pots: the beauty of running a three-pot system is switching between, say, beetroot in one pot and similarly quick-maturing turnips in the next. It keeps life interesting and gives you a range of veg similar to that in a full-sized veg garden.

You can ring the changes still further by 'zoning' your pots, enabling you to grow plants that mature at different rates in the same container. Plant a wigwam of runner beans or a bush tomato plant in the middle of each pot to grow throughout the season. Then use the outer edges for faster-maturing vegetables, sowing at staggered intervals as before, for a continuous supply.

You'll sacrifice a little in quantity compared with the single-variety system, but you'll make up for that ten times over with the sheer dazzling array of veg you suddenly find you can grow. If you've run out of peas to pick today, there are baby carrots or crinkly kale leaves or plump little turnips to roast – a kind of pick'n'mix self-sufficiency that's never, ever dull.

The following are a few 'recipe' ideas for mixed-veg pots.

A meal in a pot

Have fun combining vegetables you'd use in the same meal – like tomatoes, onions and basil for pasta sauce. Or supply yourself with annual herbs all year with a three-pot herb plot – say, combining dill, coriander and basil.

Mixed-pot recipe 1: Peas please!

This three-pot veg plot majors on moreish mangetout and podding peas. Add sweet crunchy carrots and a side order of roots for good all-round Sunday roast veg – and you could add a three-pot plot of potatoes in sacks to give you the roasties too! All are ready in around 10 to 12 weeks – so just sow an extra pot every other month to keep 'em coming.

Sugar snap peas and beetroot make perfect pot partners, and look pretty too.

Give the taller peas a central spot and provide a little support – all the varieties mentioned below are short, but they do tend to flop over their neighbours if you let them, so provide a short wigwam or poke in twiggy pea sticks among the seedlings to give them something to scramble up. Sow root vegetables at their feet, thinning every other seedling as they grow, to eat raw – as sweet a delicacy as you'll ever taste.

Pot 1: Pea 'Bingo'
Carrot 'Paris Market'
Beetroot 'Boltardy'
Pot 2: Pea 'Oregon Sugar Pod'
Carrot 'Babette'
Turnip 'Purple Top Milan'
Pot 3: Pea 'Twinkle'
Carrot 'Parmex'
Beetroot 'Golden'

The dwarf pea 'Bingo' is a prolific cropper and loves a container.

Mixed-pot recipe 2: Eat your greens

This recipe gives you three pots full of greenery – packed with vitamins, iron and sheer feel-good crunchiness – to sow three or four times a year for a continuous supply. You can really have fun with the design of this one, as there are so many different colours of kale and lettuce to play with: contrast purples and greens, or frilly leaves with flat, and you'll have a pot that's as pretty as it is practical.

Find a shady spot for it and keep it well watered, with a weekly nitrogen-rich feed (liquid seaweed works well) to keep the leaves coming. Harvest at around 6 weeks for baby leaves, or 10-12 weeks for mature plants – don't let the kale plants get too big, or they'll start to exhaust the pot's nutrient reserves. Pick leaf by leaf, so the hearts keep producing more to replace those they've lost, then each pot will crop for a good 2 months. Bring the last one indoors in late autumn to last through winter, and you'll have greens year-round.

Give peas something to scramble up, so they don't swamp their neighbours.

Mix spinach, kale and lettuce for a nutrient-packed hit of delicious leafy greens.

Pot 1: Spinach 'Bordeaux'
Kale 'Dwarf Green Curled'
Lettuce 'Pandero'

Pot 2: Spinach 'Reddy'
Kale 'Cavolo Nero'
Lettuce 'Tom Thumb'

Pot 3: Spinach 'Banjo'
Kale 'Red Russian'
Lettuce 'Nymans'

Mixed-pot recipe 3: Beefy brassicas

The bigger brassicas, such as Brussels sprouts and purple sprouting broccoli, will struggle in all but the roomiest of containers – but you don't have to do without your fix of hearty greens just because you're growing veg in pots.

Some brassicas, like kale, are perfectly happy in a container, and just grow a little smaller than they would do in the ground. But for most cabbage relatives, it's worth hunting down the new range of 'dwarf' or container varieties to try. And if you're open to new ways of growing you can include some larger brassicas too: pick the fast-growing Chinese broccoli (kailaan or stem broccoli) very young and tender, before it has a chance to bolt, and harvest conventional cabbages before they heart up properly, for loose-leaf 'greens' instead. They taste exactly the same on the plate!

Use a heavier compost than the usual shop-bought multipurpose type, such as the soil-based home-made compost (see Chapter 12, page 212) or John Innes No. 2 for this system, as cabbages and calabrese are hungry feeders, and soil-based composts hold on to nutrients for longer.

Place the taller calabrese or sprouts in the centre and tuck kale around their skirts for support, then surround this with the cabbages. Plant a container three times a year to keep the harvest fresh: most brassicas are winter stalwarts and barely flinch at frost, so leave the last one outdoors at the end of the season and just keep on picking.

Pot 1: Chinese broccoli
Kale 'Cavolo Nero'
Cabbage 'Mozart'

Pot 2: Calabrese 'Kabuki'
Kale 'Red Russian'
Cauliflower 'Igloo'

Pot 3: Brussels sprout 'Bitesize'
Kale 'Dwarf Green Curled'
Cabbage 'Samantha'

Plentiful, colourful and brimming with flavour: culinary herbs are a must for every plot.

Chapter Three

MAKE A HERB GARDEN

"Herbs make attractive features in any space, and a few basics will give you flavourings for every kind of dish."

You're probably already pretty self-sufficient in several kinds of fresh herb without even realizing it. Got a rosemary bush? That's as much as you could possibly need to flavour the lamb joint all year, with loads left over for the roast veg and summer barbecues, plus some edible flowers for salads. A single potted bay tree, and you can tick that one off the list too. Add a sage plant, a few hummocks of thyme, marjoram and parsley tucked into spare corners around the veg patch, and you've got all your kitchen flavouring sorted.

In fact, so easy is it to squeeze a few herbs into whatever space you have that it's hard to understand why anyone goes to the trouble of slogging all the way to the shops to buy evergreen herbs you could pick in a moment, all year round, outside your back door. Rosemary, for example, grows just about anywhere that's dryish, including containers. Many herbs are as attractive as they are useful: bay 'lollipops' are great formal garden sculptures; culinary sage comes in purple, variegated and green; and thyme makes a lovely ground cover, frothing with flowers in early summer.

Abundance in fresh herbs is one of those self-sufficiency luxuries. When you can reach out and grab the most generous fistful of parsley without a thought, or wander about the garden collecting a sprinkle of fresh thyme stems or a fragrant froth of fennel – that's when you feel you live a blessed life.

In this chapter I'll explain how to grow a complete starter pack of must-have herbs for every cook, from the widely used to the more subtly flavoured. They'll supply the basic flavourings for every kind of dish, whether it's meat, fish, salads or vegetables. You don't even need much space to hit herby self-sufficiency: these are plants so intensively flavoured that a few leaves can transform a whole dish, and most also grow just as happily on a windowsill or sunny patio as in the open garden. Once you've mastered the basics, you can branch out into more adventurous flavours, or maybe even start exploring the wonderful world of home-grown medicines and cosmetics too (find out more in Chapter 11!). Plus your kitchen will smell fantastic.

HERBS ALL YEAR ROUND

For herbs that die down for winter, like marjoram and tarragon, or leafy annuals such as basil and dill, you'll have to pay a little more attention when it comes to sorting year-round supplies. The traditional way of preserving herbs is through drying – but it's far from the best, as the essential oils that give herbs their flavour are fragile and easily lost. Some herbs (parsley and tarragon, for example) are awful when dried. I recruit my windowsills and freezer to the cause of capturing those lovely

Dig up a root of mint in autumn and grow it on the windowsill for winter flavour.

summery herby flavours. Dig up roots of mint, split chive clumps and pot them up to keep on the windowsill, along with some marjoram, and they'll all stay leafy for most of the winter. I back up my little windowsill herb farm by picking over my herbs in summer, while they're still growing strong, to freeze sprigs and leaves whole. Most come out almost as good as they went in.

How to freeze herbs

Freezing is my go-to method for preserving herbs in best condition. Everyone has their favourite methods: here are a few of mine.

✳ **Individual leaves** Pick leaves or sprigs in the morning, rinse lightly with water and pat dry. Lay out on a tray and put in the freezer overnight. In the morning, divide into portions, decant into individual plastic bags and return to the freezer. Use straight from frozen.

❋ **Ice cubes** Chop herbs finely and pack into an ice-cube tray until you can't get any more in. Top up with water and put in the freezer overnight. Next day, tip out the cubes into plastic bags and return them to the freezer: one cube popped into your cooking equals a teaspoon of chopped herbs.

❋ **Freezing in oil** Preserve tricky herbs like basil with minimal deterioration by painting each leaf with olive oil before placing between sheets of waxed paper. Place in the freezer overnight, then next day pop them into plastic bags and return them to the freezer until you need them.

PLANNING YOUR HERB GARDEN

The starting point for a herb garden is the same as for any other kind of food-growing: grow what you like to eat! If you have more

A well-designed herb garden makes a head-turning feature.

than a window box or space for a few pots, divide your garden into areas for your favourite meals: meat, fish and vegetables, say. Then plant key herbs for flavouring each type of cooking, and add more unusual flavours as you get more ambitious.

Herb garden designs

The luxury of a dedicated herb garden is that it gives you all your herbs a step from your back door: just nip out of the kitchen and take your pick for that evening's meal. There are lots of ways to do it. You could turn a flower border over to herbs, or go the whole way and

Pathway . . . or herb garden?

Herbal landscaping

Remove slabs or individual bricks from a path and plant low-growing herbs in the gaps, for a no-space herb supply which softens your hard landscaping too.

Clipped bay gives an instant touch of Italian style and formality.

design yourself a formal herb garden packed with all your favourite flavourings. Here are just a few ideas:

✳ **Herbs** *au naturel* An informal, mixed, cottage-style herb garden fills the garden with scent. Dramatic contrasts of texture and colour, like darkest-purple peppermint among feathery bronze fennel, mean it holds its own as an ornamental border too.
✳ **A herbal knot** Formal designs, contrasting low clipped hedges with frothing foliage, recall centuries-old traditional methods of herb-growing. The simple geometry allows you to group different types of herb together.

✳ **A herb wheel** A Native American tradition, wheels are the easiest herbal design to fit into small spaces, each division show-casing a single herb. If wagon wheels are in short supply, mark out the divisions with granite setts, brick pavers or pebbles.

Some herbs also make wonderfully scented lawn substitutes for small areas, needing no mowing and releasing a heavenly scent when you walk on them. Try a traditional chamomile lawn, using the non-flowering strain 'Trene-ague', or go for creeping thyme, *Thymus ser-pyllum*, which copes with a little shade.

FOUR HERBS FOR MEAT

You need a ballsy, distinctive flavour to hold its own with meat. The following four herbs complement meat beautifully, majoring on rich, strongly aromatic oils.

Sage (*Salvia officinalis*)

The rich, smoky flavour of culinary sage brings out the best in pork.

Partner sage with fatty foods for a rich, smoky deep flavour: pork-and-sage sausages, sage-and-onion stuffing, or roast pork belly over apples and sage. It's good with cheese too.

Growing guide

Season: Year-round evergreen.
Varieties: 'Purpurascens' for smoky purple leaves; 'Icterina' has gold-edged leaves; 'Tricolour' is purple, cream and green.
How much to grow: One plant provides more than you'll ever need. On window-sills and in containers, grow it in the largest pot you can manage and replace plants every 2-3 years. Out in the garden, a sage shrub reaches about 60cm (24") tall and wide: keep it trimmed and it'll last indefinitely.
Sowing and growing: It's easy to raise sage from seed, though only the plain green variety. You'll get a better choice if you buy a young plant. Give it a sunny, free-draining spot (in heavy soils, add grit to the planting hole).
Care: Prune back by about a third to a half in spring, to keep the plant bushy and productive.
Pests and diseases: Trouble-free as long as it's not too damp – sage rots away in soggy soils.
Harvesting and storing: Pick leaf by leaf as needed, all year round: no need to dry.

Rosemary

Handsome, evergreen rosemary is pickable at any time of year.

The richly spicy flavours of rosemary are brought out best by slow roasting. Add a few sprigs to chicken dishes, or – my personal favourite – nestle your lamb joint on a thick bed of rosemary and let the flavours infuse slowly in the oven.

Growing guide

Season: Year-round evergreen.
Species and varieties: 'Miss Jessopp's Upright' for hedging; prostrate rosemary (*Rosmarinus officinalis* Prostratus Group) for draping over walls.
How much to grow: One mature bush is plenty. The same advice applies as for sage (see page 55).
Sowing and growing: Quite tricky from seed, but cuttings take readily: root 10cm (4") sprigs in free-draining compost. Alternatively, young plants are inexpensive. Give rosemary sun and free-draining, gritty soil.
Care: A gentle haircut after flowering encourages lots of fresh young growth (and the flowers are edible too!).
Pests and diseases: The pretty but devastating rosemary beetle, striped metallic green and purple, turns new shoots into dead twigs in a trice. Pick off adults and their slug-like grubs, and if you have real problems, grow your plants under insect-proof mesh.
Harvesting and storing: Cut young sprigs at about 10cm long. The leaves don't soften on cooking, so to avoid the 'pine needles' effect, chop finely or add sprigs whole and remove before serving. Pick plants all year round.

Mint

Fuzzy-leaved apple mint makes wonderful mint sauce.

Roast lamb and mint sauce is a partnership made in heaven. Or try the tangy freshness of mint chopped into a yoghurt raita as the perfect complement to spicy Turkish beef koftas.

Growing guide

Season: Fresh from late spring to autumn (or early winter when brought indoors); dried or frozen in winter.

Species: The smooth-leaved spearmint (*Mentha spicata*) for general cooking; the fuzzy-leaved apple mint (*M. suaveolens*) for mint sauce. And there's chocolate mint (*M.* x *piperita* f. *citrata*) for baking.

How much to grow: Out in the garden, mint is best grown in containers, as it's very invasive. I grow mine in lots of big tubs – but then I use a lot of mint. On a windowsill, grow several pots, each with a different variety.

Sowing and growing: Mint is easy to grow from seed, but even easier from roots split from existing plants. Again, restrict its ambitions by growing in containers. Mint grows in sun or part shade and likes damp, rich compost.

Care: Cut back after flowering in summer to encourage new growth, and in spring each year tip it out of its pot and split up the clump, replanting one division in fresh compost to keep it productive.

Pests and diseases: Mint rust is the main enemy: look for pale, sickly spring shoots and tell-tale rusty powder on the leaves. Destroy affected plants, roots and all, and grow fresh stock somewhere else in the garden.

Harvesting and storing: Cut 10cm (4") sprigs as required. Pot up a chunk of mint plant in autumn to bring inside, and it'll stay productive well into winter. Freeze surplus sprigs whole to see you through till spring.

French tarragon

Tarragon lifts any chicken dish with its delicately aniseed flavour. It's particularly good for flavouring vinegars too. Make sure your tarragon is French (*Artemisia dracunculus*) and not the coarser, strong-flavoured Russian type (*A. dracunculoides*).

Add French tarragon, and chicken dishes go from delicious to divine.

Growing guide

Season: Summer.

Species and varieties: Just one: the savoury tang of French tarragon.

How much to grow: One plant is enough for most needs. French tarragon is happy in a pot on a windowsill and will love the extra warmth; it also enjoys a roomy, free-draining terracotta pot in a sunny spot on the patio. In the garden it makes a small, gently sprawling shrub.

Sowing and growing: French tarragon doesn't set seed in cooler climates, so grow from cuttings or buy plants in. Those available as seed are usually Russian tarragon – easier to grow, but a far inferior plant. Tarragon needs sun and poor, free-draining soil.

Care: Winter protection is essential, as tarragon is not frost-hardy. Grow it in pots and bring into a frost-free greenhouse, or (riskier) mulch the roots with straw. Divide clumps every 2 years to keep plants productive.

Pests and diseases: It can succumb to root rots in over-damp soils, but otherwise is trouble-free.

Harvesting and storing: Pick sprigs as required. It doesn't dry well; freeze surplus leaves or suffuse them in oil.

Other herbs for meat

Thyme, marjoram (often called oregano) (see pages 65-6 for both) and bay all have punchy flavours and are great low-maintenance ever-

Herb-flavoured barbecuing

Throw trimmings from your herb garden on to the barbecue during the last few moments of cooking, to infuse the meat with flavour.

greens for a sunny, free-draining spot; all are also happy in pots. Horseradish is the classic partner for beef: grow it in tall containers whether outdoors or in, as it's very invasive. Sow annual coriander (cilantro) (see Chapter 1, pages 28-30) and mustard (for the seed) in pots or straight into the ground outside.

FOUR HERBS FOR FISH

Aromatic but light-touch herbs bring out the fine flavours of fish and add a spicy twist all of their own. These four give you your go-to fish flavourings and look as delicate as they taste: tuck sprigs into foil wrapping before baking, or marinate to infuse fish with flavour.

Dill

A tall, feathery-leaved plant, dill has a piquant aniseed taste and lovely lacy yellow flowers. Lay a sprig of feathery leaves on white fish before wrapping it in foil to bake.

A couple of bay leaves infuse meaty casseroles with a lovely rich, earthy flavour.

Tall, soft and graceful, dill packs a powerful aniseedy punch in fish dishes.

Pests and diseases: Trouble-free.
Harvesting and storing: Cut the whole plant down to about 5cm (2") above ground level, and it throws up yet more wispy leaves. Collect seeds to use in cooking. Dill doesn't dry well, so freeze leaves as whole sprigs.

Fennel

Fennel is a perennial, similar in appearance to dill but with a stronger aniseed flavour. It goes with most meat and fish, but especially oily fish. Keep a pot of the seeds to chew as a natural breath freshener after meals.

Growing guide

Season: Fresh in summer; seeds in autumn.

Species and varieties: The species, *Anethum graveolens*, for the open garden; the shorter 'Compatto' for containers.

How much to grow: Flavours are strong, so you don't need much: a 1m (3') row in the garden, a sprinkling of seed in a window box or a generous potful on the patio is plenty.

Sowing and growing: Sow seed directly where it's to grow, as dill runs to flower early if transplanted. It needs sun, shelter and moist soil – and avoid growing it near fennel, as the two are related and will cross-pollinate.

Care: Keep well watered to prevent bolting (premature flowering). Dill can't compete with weeds, so hoe regularly. Allow established plants to self-seed and you'll have a colony for life, for no extra effort.

Feathery fennel has a pungent aniseed flavour.

Growing guide

Season: Fresh in summer; seeds in autumn.

Species and varieties: Comes in green (*Foeniculum vulgare*) or handsome bronze (*F. vulgare* 'Purpureum').

How much to grow: Fennel is tall and prolific once it gets going: one potful on the windowsill or patio, or an established clump in the garden, is plenty.

Sowing and growing: Either green or bronze fennel is easy from seed: once established it'll self-seed freely, so you only have to sow once. It prefers free-draining, light soil and a sunny spot. Allow 50cm (20") between plants.

Care: Generally easy to care for. Leave the architectural flower heads on through winter, as they look lovely rimed with frost. Cut down spent stalks in early spring, just before the new growth comes through.

Pests and diseases: Aphids can infest plants in summer: squish them or spray with insecticidal soap.

Harvesting and storing: Pick sprigs as required, and collect seeds once dried on the plant. The stems are also strongly flavoured: try barbecuing fish on a raft of fennel stems. Freeze foliage whole.

Parsley

Parsley goes with just about everything, and every cook should grow loads – but it really comes into its own when served with fish. Cod and parsley sauce . . . mmm, just made for each other.

Curly-leaved moss parsley stays green and plentiful right through winter.

Growing guide

Season: All year if protected in winter.

Varieties: 'Moss Green Curled' is the hardiest and prettiest. Flat-leaved parsley has a more delicate constitution but is said to have a better flavour (I disagree!).

How much to grow: You can't grow enough parsley. Luckily, it's easy to tuck in just about anywhere: fill your windowsills with pots of it and add it to every container you can spare on the patio too.

Sowing and growing: Grow from seed, sown direct, but be patient: parsley seed takes up to 6 weeks to germinate. Let a plant self-seed and you'll find that the self-sown seedlings often do better. Parsley needs cool, damp shade.

Care: Space plants 25cm (10") apart and keep weeded and watered until established. A second sowing in late summer gives you leaves to pick through winter, from pots on the windowsill or under cloches (row covers) in the garden.

Pests and diseases: Generally trouble-free. Yellowing leaves are a sign of nutrient deficiency: a quick dose of general-purpose liquid feed will help. And aphids are occasionally a nuisance: squash them or spray with insecticidal soap.

Harvesting and storing: Don't bother drying parsley leaves – they turn totally tasteless. You should be able to keep a fresh supply going most of the year, but if not, freeze leaves whole for winter use.

Caraway

Like dill and fennel, this is another tall, feathery umbellifer, resembling an elegant carrot. The leaves are good in salads, but it's the ridged seeds you really want: also known as Persian cumin, they lend warming, spicy flavours to salmon, cod and haddock. And you needn't stop there – those smoky flavours add a delicious complexity to bread and cakes, and bring out a beautiful richness in many meat dishes too.

Grow caraway for the leaves – but the seeds are where the spiciest flavour is to be found.

Growing guide

Season: Fresh in summer; seeds in autumn.

Varieties: None: just plain caraway is all you need.

How much to grow: Two or three plants provide enough seed and to spare. Caraway will grow in windowsill pots and containers on the patio, but tends to stay smaller than in the ground outdoors, so harvest it like baby leaves, then let it bolt and collect the seeds.

Sowing and growing: Seed is best sown fresh, so, if you can, collect your own and sow it straight away. Always sow direct, where you want it to grow: a sunny spot in rich, moist soil is perfect.

Care: Keep watered and weeded, and that's about it. Plants throw up their 1.5m (5') flower spikes in early summer of their second year: just allow surplus seed to drop to the ground for next year's crop.

Pests and diseases: Generally trouble-free, though you may spot a few aphids in summer: squash on sight or spray with a pyrethrum-based insecticide.

Harvesting and storing: Cut leaves for summer salads, or eat the roots – rather like skinny parsnips. But the main harvest comes when the seeds arrive in late summer the following year: gather them once brown and fully dry.

Other herbs for fish

For more unusual fish flavourings, go for the citrusy tang of lemon balm or the celery-like

Herb butter

Herb butter is a great shortcut for flavouring fish and vegetables. Cream the butter, then chop a selection of herbs – say, French tarragon, basil, chervil, parsley and thyme. Season and mix together thoroughly with the butter. Reshape it and wrap in grease-proof paper, then pop it in the fridge. Melt a knob of herb butter on to fish or grilled meat for instant flavour.

lovage – both easy-to-grow perennials. Lovage isn't a windowsill herb, though it'll manage in a large container; lemon balm is easy-going and happy indoors or out. Perennial lemon thyme and chives complement fish perfectly and are both good-natured perennials for windowsills, pots or herb gardens. Troughs sown with coriander (see Chapter 1, page 28) and shade-tolerant chervil give fistfuls of fragrantly leafy snippings too.

FOUR HERBS FOR VEGETABLES AND SALADS

Leafy, fresh flavours bring out the best in vegetable dishes, while annual herbs torn roughly into salads are as much of a must-have ingredient as the lettuce and cucumber. Here are four of my favourites.

Basil

Fresh basil torn into salads adds a touch of light, leafy spiciness.

The key herb for Mediterranean cooking, and a soulmate for tomatoes, basil is also delicious chopped into a classic pesto with olive oil and garlic, and also shredded into salads.

Growing guide

Season: Summer.
Species and varieties: 'Sweet Genovese' for classic green leaves; 'Dark Opal' for a sultry burgundy look. The small-leaved Greek basil (*Ocimum minimum*) makes a neat, plentiful mound in a pot.
How much to grow: As much as you can: basil is a herb to use with generosity. It loves to bask in the heat, so give it your warmest spot – preferably a corner of the greenhouse – or just fill sunny window-sills with pots (and fill your kitchen with fragrance).

Sowing and growing: It's easy from seed, sown in late spring to early summer. Make sowings through the year to keep a plentiful supply. Transplant the seedlings into roomy pots or into the garden, about 10cm (4") apart in full sun in rich, moist, free-draining soil.

Care: Basil grows happily in containers as long as it's well watered – in fact, it often does better, as it's liable to be munched by slugs in the garden. Even better, give it the warmth of a greenhouse. Pinch out the tips of seedlings as they grow, to encourage lots of bushy, leafy growth, and feed with a nitrogen-rich fertilizer once a week.

Pests and diseases: Slugs adore basil, so keep it well protected. Aphids often attack in the summer months too: inspect plants regularly and squish smaller colonies, or spray more persistent infestations with insecticidal soap.

Harvesting and storing: Pinch out leafy shoot tips as required – indeed, as often as possible – to stop the plants running to flower. Basil doesn't dry or freeze well, although if you paint individual leaves with oil and freeze them between wax paper, the results are usually good. But it's less fiddly just to chop the whole lot into pesto.

Marjoram (oregano)

I say marjoram, you say oregano . . . Whatever, it's one of the most useful herbs you can grow for the kitchen (and one of the easiest too).

Another essential ingredient for pasta sauces, marjoram goes beautifully with tomatoes. It also combines well with other Mediterranean herbs, such as thyme and bay for a bouquet garni. You may know this herb better as oregano, particularly if you're in the USA – the two names are used interchangeably, though there are, strictly speaking, subtle differences between the two herbs.

Growing guide

Season: Summer and autumn.
Species and varieties: The best flavour is from the tender sweet marjoram, *Origanum majorana*, usually grown as an annual. Hardy perennial marjoram (or oregano), *O. vulgare*, is easier and comes in a huge range of varieties.
How much to grow: As much as you can: marjoram is your go-to herb for any Mediterranean cooking. Half a dozen plants in the veg garden, a generous pot indoors or a window box, or a sizeable potful on the patio keeps you well supplied.
Sowing and growing: Easy to grow from seed sown in spring, or divide established clumps. Buy young plants if you want a named variety. Plant outside in a warm, sunny, free-draining spot. Marjoram is also happy in pots.
Care: Marjoram is easy to look after, drought-tolerant and does well even in poor soils. Lift and divide clumps every 2 or 3 years to keep them young, and trim back spent flowers in autumn.
Pests and diseases: None to speak of: mint rust (see page 57) can affect marjoram too, but only rarely. Destroy affected plants and grow new stock in a different spot in the garden.
Harvesting and storing: Snip away leaves as required. Marjoram dries well: pick in summer before the plant flowers, and spread out on trays to dry for a couple of weeks before storing in an airtight jar.

Thyme

This classic Mediterranean staple is a herb-garden must-have. Pop a sprig or two of thyme in just about any pasta sauce, or in soups, stews and casseroles, for a deliciously warm, rich flavour.

The pretty flowers of thyme are adored by bees.

Growing guide

Season: Year-round evergreen.

Species and varieties: Common thyme (*Thymus vulgaris*) is plentiful; lemon thyme (*T. citriodorus*) has a lovely citrusy twist; broad-leaved thyme (*T. pulegioides*) has larger leaves.

How much to grow: At least half a dozen plants – more if you can – as you'll want to cut plenty. A generous pot- or window-box-ful indoors, or a handful of containers on the patio, should keep you well stocked year-round.

Sowing and growing: Thyme is easily raised from seed, though for named varieties it's best to buy in young plants. It grows in practically zero soil (the creeping *Thymus herba-barona* – caraway thyme – favours cracks in walls), so you just need to provide a sunny spot and poor, sharply draining soil.

Care: Easy to look after, though beware neighbouring plants: if thyme becomes overshadowed or crowded it will quickly languish. Trim plants gently after flowering to encourage fresh new growth.

Pests and diseases: Trouble-free.

Harvesting and storing: Snip sprigs away with scissors as required. Thyme stops growing in winter, so go easy on harvesting in colder months: bring a plant indoors to keep picking more heavily, or dry your surplus.

Chervil

It's a mystery to me why chervil is so rarely grown. One of the few herbs that loves shade, it's untroubled by pests, and its dainty, filigree leaves are one of the *fines herbes* much prized in France, adding a warm, mildly aniseedy flavour to autumn salads.

Growing guide

Season: Fresh from early autumn through winter and into early spring.

Species and varieties: Ordinary chervil, *Anthriscus cerefolium*, does for most requirements, though 'Curled' has prettily ruffled leaves.

How much to grow: As much as you can – three large troughs sown successively from late summer will keep you going through till spring. Indoors, fill a window box and keep cutting for a continuous supply.

Sowing and growing: Chervil hates the sun and will bolt the moment it gets too warm or dry. So to keep it leafy and productive, find it a cool, damp and shady spot and sow it late in the season, from late summer or early autumn. Once you've got a clump going you can always let it self-seed: flowers appear the following summer and scatter seed happily about, so you never need be without it. Just transplant the seedlings carefully, while they're still young, to where you want them to grow.

Care: With a little protection over winter – a cloche will do, or, if growing in containers, just move them into a sheltered spot – chervil stays leafy right through winter. In mild winters you can probably even dispense with the cloche.

Pests and diseases: Chervil is refreshingly problem-free. You might get the occasional aphid, but even that's rare.

Harvesting and storing: Snip away leaves with scissors about 5cm (2") above soil level. Fresh is the only way to enjoy chervil: drying or freezing will clobber those delicate flavours. Luckily, being a winter-productive herb, it's only summer you have to worry about, and at that time of year there are lots of other herbs that make good stand-ins.

Other herbs for vegetables and salads

Salad burnet has delicate leaves with a hint of cucumber: it's an easy-to-grow perennial for pots and windowsills as well as in the garden. Coriander is deliciously warm and spicy snipped fresh into salads (see Chapter 1, pages 28-30, for details). To add a little tang to your salads, turn to chives and sorrel (which has a lemony taste): both come back year after year and are happy in pots.

The leafy summer savory tastes a little like thyme and is a must for bringing out the flavour in broad beans (fava beans): sow it annually, in troughs for windowsills and patios, or outdoors. And what would new potatoes be without fresh mint? Grow it in pots, whether indoors or out, to keep its invasive tendencies in check (see page 57 for details).

Herbs are so versatile they can grow just about anywhere.

Sweet, glistening redcurrants can be grown in the most bijou of gardens.

PLANT A MINI ORCHARD

> *"Bountiful home-grown fruit is one of the best rewards of self-sufficiency. And you can grow it on a patio, up fences . . . even on a windowsill."*

Well, obviously I don't mean *that* kind of orchard. Not if you're thinking big field, ancient gnarly apple trees, blossom humming with bees. No: I'm talking twenty-first-century orchards. The kind you can fit into a city back yard, or a few pots on the patio. It's time we rethought our tradition-soaked ideas about how you're supposed to grow fruit. Things have changed since the 1930s, when Lord de Rothschild advised that "no garden, however small, should be without its 2 acres of woodland". Nowadays, you don't even need a fruit cage. Grow redcurrants up your walls and use your apples as fencing instead.

In fact, what with blowsy froths of blossom in spring; luscious, fat berries in autumn and often crimson-and-ochre displays of autumn leaf colour too, it's a mystery why anyone would want to hide fruit away behind a wall of netting. Bring it out for all to admire: plant plums among your

Apple trees underplanted with wallflowers at the National Trust's Barrington Court in Somerset.

You can make blackcurrant jam and summer puddings and still give your surplus away. And of course it's all completely organic, and practically free.

THE 'HUNGRY GAP'

There's a spell from early spring (when the stored apples run out) to early summer (when the first gooseberries arrive) when there simply isn't much fresh fruit around. Rhubarb is the only fruit at this time of year – and, delicious and versatile though it is (rhubarb crumble cake is a big favourite in our house), it's hardly the same as grabbing an apple. But most berry fruit freezes well, emerging almost as good as fresh-picked – so just resign yourself to the hardship of heaps of saved raspberries, blackberries or tayberries instead for a while. Tough, this self-sufficiency, isn't it?

In addition to freezing, there are a few other tricks for beating the hungry gap in your fruit supply:

❋ **Choose late-maturing fruit** Include a good range of varieties that take most of the season to produce their fruit, as these are the ones that store the longest. 'Winter Nelis' pears, 'Laxton's Superb' and 'Spartan' apples, and quinces all keep for ages.

❋ **Force rhubarb** In late winter, after frost, cover a fast-maturing rhubarb such as 'Timperley's Early' with a black dustbin to exclude light. In the dark, rhubarb stems are slender and exquisitely sweet. Let the crowns rest for a year before you force them again, to give them a chance to get their strength back.

poppies and apples alongside alstroemerias. If you have room to grow any plants, you have room for fruit. It's that simple.

The orchards you'll find in this chapter may be pint-sized, but all are productive. There's one for every size of garden: I'll explain how to squeeze fruit into your garden so subtly that you'll hardly even notice it's there; how to turn your patio into a container orchard, dripping with glistening strawberries and plump purple plums; festoon your wall and fences with vertically grown fruit; and even how to grow fruit when you have no garden at all.

Home-grown fruit is almost overwhelmingly generous – the ultimate proof that self-sufficiency is the luxury choice. Raspberries don't come in stingy little plastic punnets: they come in huge brimming bowlfuls, and the kids grab handfuls for after-school snacks.

❋ **Force strawberries** Dig up strawberry plants in late winter, after the frost has been at them, and pot them up to bring into a cool greenhouse so they flower a month or two early. You'll need to hand-pollinate them, as there are few insects around so early: just dab each flower in turn with a soft artist's brush.

❋ **Preserve your fruit** Get your fruity fix from juices, dried and bottled fruits, just-defrosted frozen berries and – my personal favourite – fruit 'leathers': purées dried slowly in the oven (spread on a lined baking tin and bake overnight or for 8-12 hours at 60°C/140°F) then sliced into sticky sweets that you don't have to feel guilty for liking.

Stop thinking of fruit trees or bushes as just edible, and start looking at them as ornamental.

Apples ripening nicely.

THE SMALL-GARDEN ORCHARD

If you have any outdoor space at all, you're halfway to having your orchard already. In handkerchief-sized gardens, where every plant really counts, fruit ticks all the boxes: space-efficient and low-maintenance, yet contributing beauty and a bountiful harvest too.

Stop thinking of fruit trees or bushes as just edible, and start looking at them as ornamental plants. Most have attractive qualities, whether it's blossom, prettily coloured bark, good autumn colour or bright-coloured berries. Some have it all. Choose them just as you'd pick out other perennials or shrubs, and your orchard blends into the smallest garden so effectively that you become self-sufficient in fruit almost without realizing. This is your hidden orchard: you get to have a pretty garden, but you can eat it too.

Apple blossom as pretty as any garden flowers.

Fruit (and nut) trees

When choosing a fruit tree for a small garden you'll have the words 'compact' and 'year-round interest' at the top of your wish list.

Well, that describes most fruit trees. Quinces, for example, reach no more than 5m (16') tall, with charming open pink blossom in spring, butter-yellow autumn colour and fruits that perfume the air for miles. Crab apples are great value: frothy white spring blossom, brilliant autumn leaves and fruits like miniature apples (the variety 'John Downie' is best for scrummy jelly-making). Even ordinary old apple blossom is better appreciated when brought into the main garden: those on smaller, semi-dwarfing rootstocks like MM106 don't get much taller than 4m (13'). See pages 74-83 for more on compact fruit trees and bushes, while more detailed advice about fruit trees can be found in *The Fruit Tree Handbook* (see Resources section).

Nut trees too make beautiful small-garden trees. Cobnuts, the closely related filbert and, in warmer climates, almonds all have lovely blossom and give plentiful harvests.

Fruiting shrubs

Autumn berries are easily as colourful as flowers: little clustered droplets of red, orange or, in the case of the beautyberry, *Callicarpa bodinieri*, metallic purple.

But you can't eat beautyberries. So grow blueberries instead: their burnished near-black fruits are every bit as gorgeous. Blackcurrants add handsome ramrod-straight stems, whitecurrants hold their berries in translucent clusters, and richly flavoured Japanese wineberries (*Rubus phoenicolasius*) make good raspberry substitutes.

Edible hedging

Forget boring beech, box and laurel: give your hedges an extra dimension by using fruit plants instead. For a formal look, plant a row of blackcurrants or gooseberries. For the full-throttle edible hedge experience, go for a mishmash of fruits to keep you foraging right through winter. Weave roses (*Rosa rugosa* varieties, for hips) through gooseberries, elaeagnus and *Cornus mas* – a dogwood with brilliant edible red fruit. Add myrobalan plums (*Prunus cerasifera*) and blackthorn for sloes, and you'll have not just a hedge but a dense edible barrier.

Edible edging

When you're gardening with no space to spare, dedicated strawberry beds are a luxury you can't afford. So edge your flower beds

Eat your ornamentals

Lots of garden trees and shrubs that are sold as ornamentals in fact have edible fruit. Try the blue-black fruits of the juneberry (*Amelanchier canadensis*) or the big red berries of the strawberry tree (*Arbutus unedo*). Of those familiar garden shrubs, you could try the blocky purple fuchsia fruits (see page 89), rich elaeagnus berries or the slatey-blue mahonia 'grapes'.

The berries of mahonia – also known as Oregon grapes – are tart but delicious.

with them instead. Strawberries' lush, largely evergreen foliage is the perfect ground cover, topped with pretty white flowers in early summer and those delectable red berries.

Ring the changes on variety with early, mid-season and late types, to extend the season right through summer; or try an 'ever-bearing' variety – bearing smaller flushes of fruit from early summer to early autumn. For something really different, 'Toscana' is an eye-catching everbearer with bright pink flowers.

Fruity formal features

Clip your edibles into shape (after they've fruited) and make a smart formal feature to frame or define your pathways. Whitecurrants and gooseberries can be trained into lollipops (see page 87): plant them in pairs either side of a path or as a single focal point in a border, underplanted with low-growing perennials. Or stand them each side of your front door in terracotta containers. They make a nice change from clipped box, and you get the added bonus of delicately pretty and tasty clusters of berries.

Strawberries make a pretty edible edging plant.

THE CONTAINER ORCHARD

Even when a patch of open ground is a luxury and you're restricted to containers on a patio, you can still grow fruit. In fact, the first fruit I ever grew was in a pot: a lovely ornate clay thing with pockets moulded into the side, to smother in lush leafy strawberry plants. It was a revelation. Strawberries actually grow really well in containers, relishing the warmth of terracotta and producing gleaming bunches of fruit; every berry clean and unblemished by soil or slugs. I still mourn my strawberry planter, lost in a close encounter between a large dog and a tennis ball (an occupational hazard for containers in my garden), but I still grow strawberries in big tin baths. Just as good, and a lot more dog-proof.

These days you can grow apples, pears, peaches and cherries in containers too, grafted on to size-restricting dwarfing rootstocks – often naturally columnar 'Ballerina' varieties or 'minarette' trees – vertically trained cordons – with such small roots that they're perfectly happy in a pot. With so little in the way of branches to worry about, they concentrate on fruiting instead, so the crops can be quite prolific.

New compact varieties of other fruit are turning up every year too, as modern breeding innovations concentrate on the space-strapped modern gardener. Recent breakthrough arrivals include container varieties of raspberries ('Ruby Beauty'), blackcurrants ('Blackbells') and redcurrants ('Stanza'), as well as patio quinces and medlars.

Some fruit are just naturally content in containers: figs fruit better if they have their roots constrained, and blueberries are often happier in a pot, especially if the alternative is super-alkaline chalky soil like mine. They need ericaceous (acid) conditions, so for many people the only option is containers of ericaceous compost.

Growing fruit in containers is worth considering even if you do have a garden. If you need to move house, your orchard just comes with you. And, because they're portable, you can grow much more delicate species: when you can move them out of the rain, apricots and peaches escape the dreaded peach leaf curl, and their early-season blossoms don't get clobbered by a late frost. And potted fruit looks so pretty, especially combined with low-growing perennials and grasses, or scented-leaf geraniums.

Star container performers

Your potted orchard can be at least as varied as the garden sort, and you can harvest an astonishingly large fruit bowl if you stick to

Lemon trees fruit well in containers – even in chilly old Britain.

That's the summer's puddings sorted then!

these star varieties, which perform especially well in containers. For details of how to train your plants, see pages 85-7.

Apples

Apples are very amenable things and don't mind a very restricted environment. Grow them as mini apple trees, no more than 2m (6'6") tall, or train them into single-stem minarettes (vertical cordons).

Growing tips: Choose a slow-growing, dwarfing rootstock: M27 or M26 are ideal.

Stake minarettes, and grow at least two varieties, chosen from the same pollination group, to make sure you get a bumper crop.
Varieties: 'Adam's Pearmain' and 'Sunset' are particularly happy in pots (both are late-cropping; pollination group 3).

Blackcurrants

Upright, handsome and easy to grow, blackcurrants are a staple crop in fruit cages everywhere. But choose a more compact variety and you can have those gleaming ebony berries in containers too.

Fruity jargon-buster

Here are a few of the sometimes-confusing terms you might come across as you strike out into the flavoursome world of fruit-growing.

Fruiting spurs: Little clusters of buds, usually halfway along a stem, quite fat and very different from the elongated, single or paired leaf buds. Be careful not to prune off the fruiting spurs, or you're cutting off your fruit! Most fruit trees are spur-bearing – carrying fruit along the length of a branch – but some, like 'Bramley's Seedling' apples, are tip-bearing – bearing fruit on the ends of branches.

Pollination group: Many fruit trees (especially apples, pears and plums) can't pollinate themselves, so they need a pollination 'partner' nearby. But some fruit trees flower early; others late – and if two aren't flowering together, they can't cross-pollinate. So choose partners that flower at the same time – in the same 'pollination group'.

Primocane: Fruiting on this season's wood: often used of autumn-fruiting raspberries, and other cane fruit such as tayberries. Summer-fruiting raspberries, which fruit on last year's wood, are called 'floricane'.

Rootstock: Most fruit trees are formed by grafting a variety selected for its fruiting ability on to the roots of a tree selected for its natural growing size. The choice of rootstock largely determines the eventual size of the tree. The rootstock should be indicated on the plant label, so pay attention to this when choosing your tree.

Winter chilling: Most hardy fruit needs a spell of cold weather to initiate flowering and therefore fruiting. After a warm winter, crops of fruit such as strawberries, apples and blackcurrants will be naturally poor, as they haven't had enough cold weather. Ideally, they need over a month at temperatures below 7°C (44°F) to do well.

Growing tips: Don't keep blackcurrants too warm – they need frost, at least 3 weeks below 7°C (44°F) in winter, to produce those vitamin-packed berries. Re-pot every 2 or 3 years to keep plants healthy.

Varieties: Container-designed varieties include 'Blackbells'. 'Ben Connan' and 'Ben Sarek' are more traditional compact blackcurrants, also suitable for pots.

Blueberries

This is the poster plant for fruit bushes that double as handsome garden shrubs. Neat and low-growing, with sumptuous autumn colour

Grow blueberries in pots of ericaceous compost and you can give them the damp, acidic soil conditions they like.

Recycle your Christmas tree

Mulch blueberries with the needles and shredded branches from your Christmas tree. Like any mulch, it will keep down weeds and lock in moisture – plus it's naturally acidic, giving your blueberries the low-pH conditions they adore.

and blue-black berries, it's hard to beat. Just remember to pick the fruit after you've finished admiring it!

Growing tips: Grow at least two plants, for really good pollination and the heaviest crops. They need acidic soil, so use ericaceous (lime-free) compost, and keep them damp but not waterlogged.

Varieties: 'Top Hat' is naturally dwarfing; 'Northblue' and 'Bluecrop' top out at about 1.2m (4').

Caring for your potted orchard

Fruit trees and bushes in pots need more attention than those in the ground. Follow this checklist of care for best results.

✳ Use roomy containers – fruit trees and bushes need 45-60cm (18"-24") diameter, while wide and low is better for the shallower-rooted straw-berries (unless you have a purpose-designed strawberry planter of course). Three or four strawberries fit into a 30cm (12")-diameter container.

✳ A fruit plant is in its container for the long haul, so give it compost with some extra welly to keep it sustained. An equal mix of a soil-based compost such as John Innes No. 3, garden topsoil and multipurpose potting compost provides good anchorage and a plentiful reservoir of nutrients.

✳ Re-pot into a size larger each spring, until you can't manage the container any more, then top-dress the pot instead: scrape off the top 5cm (2") of compost and replace it with fresh, plus a helping of slow-release fertilizer.

✳ Container plants are completely dependent on you for food and water, so be generous. Late spring to early summer is the critical stage, when trees and shrubs are burgeoning into leaf and blossom.

Remember to protect your harvest! Net berry fruit as soon as it starts colouring up, to keep the birds off.

✳ Roots are insulated when they grow in the ground, but in a container the frost can get through – and even if the above-ground part of the plant can cope with frost, its roots can't. So wrap your potted orchard up in winter. Surround the pot with a layer of newspaper or fleece, topped with bubble wrap. Or just bring the pots into cool, dry shelter: a garage or shed works well – but don't bring them into the house, as central heat-ing is too warm and dry (though radiator-free conservatories or porches are ideal for warm-climate plants like citrus).

Citrus such as oranges, lemons and limes are very happy – and easier to look after – in pots.

Citrus fruit

Citrus fruits, such as lemons, grapefruits, limes and calamondin oranges (*Citrus* x *microcarpa* – a miniature orange, great for containers), are best grown in pots in cooler climates, as they're frost-tender. Citrus in pots is also a very classy look, bringing a touch of Versailles into the humblest back garden.

Growing tips: Citrus won't tolerate temperatures below -5°C (23°F), so move plants indoors for winter, but do this very gradually, or they'll drop their leaves. They take over a year to produce fruit from their scented winter flowers (see also Chapter 10, pages 182-3).
Species and varieties: Lemons fruit particularly reliably; the waisted leaves of kaffir limes are essential flavouring for Thai cooking.

Figs

Put a fig in the ground and it turns into a triffid, throwing up massive suckers and a forest of green leafery – but not much fruit. Restrict its

Choose the best varieties for containers, and you'll harvest an astonishingly large fruit bowl.

roots in a container, and it's much more docile (and productive).

Growing tips: Train against a wall if possible, to expose the fruit to maximum sunlight. Prune in early summer, taking side shoots back to five leaves from the main stems.
Varieties: 'Brown Turkey' is the go-to fig for cooler areas; 'Rouge de Bordeaux' has outstanding flavour.

Gooseberries

Tart, bristly and bursting with flavour, gooseberries are the first proper fruit to ripen, from early summer onwards. I honour their arrival with the biggest gooseberry fool I can muster.

Growing tips: Train plants, against a wall or as a lollipop, and the dreaded gooseberry sawfly will have nowhere to hide from birds. These little green larvae are capable of stripping a mature bush of foliage in days. And of

Elegantly fan-trained figs at the National Trust's Tyntesfield in Somerset.

Gorgeous fuzzy scarlet berries, just about to mature, on my rampantly productive wineberry.

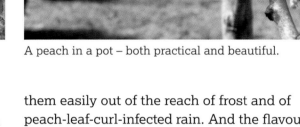

A peach in a pot – both practical and beautiful.

course trained plants look pretty too.

Varieties: 'Invicta' is rock-solid reliable. For a wine-red, sweet dessert goosegog, try 'Whinham's Industry'.

Japanese wineberries

This raspberry relative is seductively pretty, but the soft scarlet bristles and jewel-like fruit hide a constitution of steel. The berries are mouthwatering, tart and sweet at the same time, and there are plenty of them.

Growing tips: Give it a sturdy wigwam to scramble up and train stems round in a 45-degree spiral to keep them neat. Trim out fruited stems in winter, tying new growth back in for next year's fruit.

Varieties: None (yet), just the species, *Rubus phoenicolasius*.

Peaches

Growing peaches and nectarines in containers has definite compensations: you can move them easily out of the reach of frost and of peach-leaf-curl-infected rain. And the flavour of a just-picked peach is a transcendent experience.

Growing tips: Peaches don't come on rootstocks, so choose a naturally dwarfing variety, growing to about 2m (6'6"). They need little pruning: just pinch out every other fruit, leaving 15-20 on the tree to get to a decent size.

Varieties: 'El Dorado' and 'Bonanza' are naturally small; 'Babcock', grown on a dwarfing rootstock for containers, is white-fleshed.

Redcurrants

This is my favourite summer-pudding ingredient, with the prettiest berries. The translucent, scarlet, bead-like fruit are borne in long, elegant strings. Redcurrants are also drought-tolerant, making them ideal fruit bushes for containers.

Growing tips: Prune into a goblet shape in winter, keeping an open centre to let the air

Strawberries are easily tucked around the edges of containers.

Espaliers like this one at the National Trust's Barrington Court are strikingly architectural.

circulate – or train against a wall in a double-U cordon, for a lovely architectural feature.
Varieties: 'Stanza' is more compact and doesn't mind pots; 'Redstart' is excellent for training.

Strawberries

Just as good (if not better) in pots than in the ground, strawberries work everywhere in a no-garden orchard. Tuck them under your potted fruit trees, make a feature with a purpose-designed strawberry tub, or hang them up in baskets.

Growing tips: Give them your sunniest spot and plant a range of varieties to crop at different times. Replace plants with new ones every 3 years, to keep the yields high (see Chapter 5, page 102, for more details).
Varieties: 'Mara des Bois' has superb flavour; 'Cambridge Favourite' has heavier crops but for a shorter time.

VERTICAL ORCHARDS

Run out of room on the ground? Then the only way is up. Even if you have only a tiny yard to play with, you can use walls, fences, pergola posts, sheds, greenhouses and of course the house walls to grow fruit. All you need to do is train it to grow where you want it to.

A taste of the tropical

Expand your range with exotic fruits in pots: Chilean guavas, bananas ('Dwarf Cavendish' fruits even in cooler climates), melons and even pineapples are all possible in containers in a greenhouse or conservatory.

Fans are an elegant way to train plums, as here at the National Trust's Barrington Court.

The basic principle behind training fruit is to minimize green, vegetative growth – the kind that makes a plant grow bigger – while maximizing fruit production. Trained fruit takes up much less room. You can grow a whole orchard's worth along a single house wall: four cordon apples, grown at 45-degree angles against a wall, fit into a border just 2.4m (8') long.

Get creative and draw ladders, fans and goblets on your fences, outlined in fruit-laden branches, or criss-cross cordons into a diamond-shaped trellis. Trained trees make handsomely architectural shapes in winter; and in summer a redcurrant trained into a double-U cordon – like a candelabra dripping with clear scarlet beads – is a fine sight. For something even more classy, try cherries or plums trained into decorative fans. Fig trees fruit better when trained, and you can persuade quinces, medlars and even mulberry trees into elegant multi-tiered espaliers.

Supports are crucial for trained fruit: make a framework of wires starting 45cm (18") from the ground, then at 30cm (12") intervals up the wall. Attach at each end to braced 8cm (3¼")-diameter end posts using vine eyes, or omit the posts and screw the wires directly into the wall using rawlplugs. For a longer stretch, add further uprights every 1m (3'3").

Fan-trained trees need an additional support framework of canes, tied in to the horizontal supports in a fan arrangement, to give you the framework you're training the new branches on to. An open-weave trellis also works, but you may need additional canes or wires to begin with, while you establish a good shape.

Start with young plants for your vertical orchard. For tree fruit, buy a 'feathered maiden' – a 1-year-old tree with its side branches still attached. Or you could take the easy option and buy a pre-trained tree, usually 2 or 3 years old, so it's already started to take the shape you want.

Trained fruit forms

Pruning is an essential skill to learn if you're growing fruit in smaller spaces, and especially if you want to train your plants. It's a twice-a-year job: once in the middle of summer to encourage fruiting buds, and again in winter to guide and control growth.

For the first 4 or 5 years, the purpose of pruning is to form a good shape. Then, once the tree or bush has filled the available frame-work, it becomes a matter of keeping the plant healthy and productive, and trimming it back into bounds.

It may sound fearsomely technical, but actually training fruit isn't difficult, as long as you take your time and keep stepping back to check you're still on the right track. Do plenty of research first (helpful books on the subject include *The Fruit Tree Handbook* – see Resources – or you could join a fruit-training workshop at a local horticultural college or garden), and then just have a go. Here are a few of the easiest trained fruit forms to try at home.

basal cluster

The basal cluster. Side shoots grow in two stages: first a 'basal cluster' of two or three leaves, then the main leaves spaced apart. In the following instructions, when I say, for example, "prune to three leaves", this means three leaves *above* the basal cluster, as shown above. For simplicity, the basal cluster isn't shown in the following diagrams.

- -

Fan

Trained flat against a wall, the fan's branches are selected to 'fan out' evenly across the space (a framework of canes tied in to horizontal wires helps guide the shape). It takes up a similar space to espaliers (see page 86).
Best for: cherries, plums.

Getting started: Cut back the leading shoot to about 45cm (18"), just above two well-chosen side shoots, one each side. Then tie two canes on to your support wires at 45° angles, and train these two laterals on to them as they grow.

As it grows: Choose two well-spaced shoots from the top of each branch, and one from the bottom, and train them along more canes attached to the support wires. Remove completely any shoots growing in the wrong direction. Pinch out all side shoots at three or four leaves, then after harvest prune them right back to the basal cluster: these will be your fruiting spurs.

Espalier

Trained flat against a wall in a ladder-like formation, the espalier has pairs of branches emerging from the stem at 30cm (12") intervals.

Allow 3.5-4.5m (11'6"-14'6") of 1.8m (6')-high fence per plant.
Best for: apples, pears.

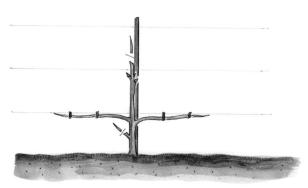

Getting started: Tie the stem to a cane, and cut it back to just above three shoots. Tie two into support wires to form the first two 'arms'; the third will make a new leader (main shoot), as shown. Train the leader up the cane, and in the next 2 years repeat for the next two tiers.

As it grows: Once all your tiers are started, cut back the leader to just above the topmost wire. Each summer, prune side shoots to two or three leaves (these will be your fruiting spurs) and remove entirely any unwanted shoots growing from the main trunk or into the wall.

- -

Cordon

The cordon is a single stem, with side shoots trimmed back to a couple of buds to encourage only fruiting spurs. It is usually grown at

45 degrees (or more) to the vertical, as this prompts the plant to produce more fruit.
Best for: apples, gooseberries, redcurrants.

Getting started: Plant the tree at a 45° angle and add a cane for support (and to keep the stem straight), tied in to the support wires. Leave the leader and any short side shoots unpruned to begin with, but trim back any that are longer than 10cm (4") to three buds.

As it grows: Keep tying the main stem in to the cane, and once it reaches the top wire, snip out the leader. Each summer, cut back all the side shoots to two or three leaves; if there are any sub-shoots growing from these spurs, prune these harder, to one or two leaves.

Stepover cordon

Essentially this is a horizontal cordon, with a single branch trained at a right angle about 45cm (18") above the ground, and side shoots pruned back to two or three buds to encourage plenty of fruit.
Best for: apples.

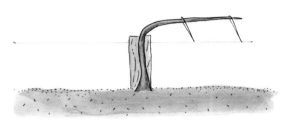

Getting started: Fix a single wire about 45cm (18") above the ground to sturdy vertical posts. Plant your tree by one of the posts, tie it in, and then spend the whole of the first season gradually pulling the stem down to the horizontal by tying it in ever-more tightly along its length.

As it grows: From the second summer, start to cut back the side shoots to two or three leaves – just like pruning a cordon. Keep tying the leading shoot in to its wire as it grows, then, when it's as long as you want it, cut out the end just beyond a side shoot.

Lollipop

Also known as a 'standard', this is a clean, single stem with all the growth concentrated in a neat globe perched on top, in a classic lollipop shape. It's great for freeing up the ground underneath bush fruit for other planting.
Best for: gooseberries, whitecurrants, redcurrants.

Getting started: Choose a bush with a strong upright leading shoot (these can be difficult to find, as many nurseries prune them out). Support this with a 1m (3') cane, and tie it in as it grows. Prune out all side shoots completely, leaving just the top-most knot of leaves growing.

As it grows: Once the main stem reaches the height you want (but no more than 1.2m/4'), select five main branches to form an open, bowl-shaped crown. Each year, shorten these main stems by a third in late summer, and then in winter prune back their side shoots to two or three buds.

THE NO-GARDEN ORCHARD

Even when you haven't got so much as a yard or fence to call your own, you can still have an orchard.

It won't be large, of course – self-sufficiency in, say, apples or plums is probably out of your reach. But even a few window boxes will give you a respectable supply of strawberries for some months in summer. And there are real delights to be had from indoor fruit: ditch the house plants and grow fruit trees instead, and you'll fill your home with the scents of orange and lemon blossom. Soft fruits to try in large containers, even as houseplants, include cape gooseberries, fuchsias and Chilean guavas.

If you're blessed with a frost-free conservatory, your fruit bowl begins to look positively Caribbean: edible passionfruit, grapevines and even figs ('Petite Negri' is a compact variety) are all possible in light, airy, warm rooms indoors. If you have access to the open air – on a balcony, say – you can expand even further: dwarf peaches like 'El Dorado', patio (dwarf) quinces and medlars (see Chapter 5, page 103 for more on quinces). They all need a cool spell, below 7°C (44°F) to thrive, so aren't suitable as houseplants, but will happily live on a balcony or flat roof extension.

Access to the outdoors is appreciated even by plants from the tropics, so, if at all possible, give your houseplant orchard a holiday somewhere warm and sheltered outdoors for at least a few weeks in high summer – they seem to really pick up after a spell in the fresh air.

And of course bees are somewhat scarce inside the average house or flat (bar the odd lost soul bumbling in through an open window). So you have to do their job for them, if your indoor orchard is to bear fruit.

Hand-pollinating is nowhere near as complicated as it sounds. All you need is a soft artist's paintbrush: once your indoor-grown strawberries, nectarines or lemons blossom, just dab the end into each flower in turn. You'll need to repeat this once a week while the plant is flowering. Of course you don't have to hand-pollinate self-fertile varieties (while figs are parthenocarpic, producing their fruit without any pollination at all).

Five fruits for an indoor orchard

Forget dull old palms and orchids, and add a whole extra dimension to your houseplants. These five are perfectly happy growing indoors and should give you a respectable harvest of exotic home-grown fruit to enjoy.

Cape gooseberries

These are those sweet, golden, cherry-like fruits that come in an elegant papery lantern. You often come across them as garnishes in posh restaurants – but grow your own and you can have bowlfuls to snack on every evening. They make a rather sprawling plant, around 60cm (24") wide and high, but they thrive in large containers (at least 45cm/18" diameter) in a conservatory or sunny front room. They're easy to raise from seed and are self-fertile.

Chilean guavas

This pretty yet robust little evergreen shrub sports lily-of-the-valley-like flowers followed by fruits like pink blueberries, but with a hint of strawberry in the flavour. Chilean guavas thrive in containers, but they must have ericaceous (acidic) compost. They don't mind the low light levels indoors, though they'll crop better the more sun you can give them. A regular liquid feed helps encourage plenty of fruit, but they won't need pollinating, as they're self-fertile.

Fuchsia berries

Yes, you read that right: fuchsias may be better known as star turns in summer hanging baskets, but their fruits are edible. Most ornamental varieties have been bred for flowers, so their fruits can be disappointing: but there's now an increasing range of fuchsias sold specifically for their fruits, including 'FuchsiaBerry' and Censation® 'Juice Berry'. They make delightful houseplants, cascading fetchingly over the edge of their pots – but give them the sunniest spot you can manage, and keep them well watered and regularly fed. They're partially self-fertile, but you'll get heavier crops if you grow more than one and hand-pollinate the flowers.

Lemons

In a cool climate, growing lemons and other citrus fruits as houseplants is by far the best way to fill your house with delicious perfume from their pretty white scented winter blossoms (see also pages 81 and 182-3). Picking the right spot is vital: all citrus suffer in too

Citrus trees will enjoy a summer holiday outdoors.

much heat and dryness, so find a cool, sunny room away from radiators. Keep humidity high by misting or standing the plant on a saucer of gravel filled with water. Feed with specialist citrus feed, and move outdoors in warmer weather if you can.

Strawberries

Probably the easiest of fruit for your indoor orchard, as happy in a pot as in the ground, you'll get strawberries weeks ahead of everyone else if you're growing them in the warmth of a sunny windowsill. Force an early-cropping variety like 'Honeoye' indoors from February, hand-pollinating as the flowers appear, and you'll be enjoying the fruit from late May. Strawberries need some time outdoors to crop well the next year, though, so pop them outside for winter or grow them in a window box where the frost can get at them.

All the plenty of the garden can be yours if you eat in tune with the seasons.

Chapter Five

EAT WITH THE SEASONS

> *"Grow your own, and you get back in touch with the natural world. Eat seasonally, and food becomes exciting again."*

When you're head down in the office bashing away at a keyboard while simultaneously phoning the garage, scribbling shopping lists and wondering what to cook for the kids' tea, you'd be for-given for not looking up for long enough to notice the passing of the seasons. But being aware of where you are in the year is a fundamental part of getting back in touch with the world around you. Plus it's compul-sory if you're growing your own food: knowing what stage your crops are at, when to reap and when to sow – they're all essential skills for the self-sufficient gardener. Trouble is, what with air freight and refrigerated storage, we've largely abolished the seasons. We can just go shopping to eat strawberries in winter and asparagus in autumn. How very dull!

Life in my kitchen, stocked from the garden outside, is a series of highs. We gorge on asparagus in spring, because we know that by summer it'll be gone till next year. Early summer means gooseberry fool; late summer

Hearty brassicas like Savoy cabbages lead the winter line-up.

and scatter raspberries by the fistful on everything from cereal to yoghurt to ice cream all summer: you'll still have plenty left over. Nobody said self-sufficiency had to be difficult, after all.

You need a garden to grow some seasonal delicacies: asparagus, for example, never grows happily in containers. But there are loads of seasonal treats to enjoy from pots, including blueberries, mangetout peas, strawberries and new potatoes. In this chapter you'll discover how to convert your eating to fit the seasons, as well as some real seasonal highlights to enjoy from your garden.

and we're eating the biggest, lushest cheesecake I can muster, smothered in plump blackcurrants. I look forward to them so much I have dreams about them.

Eating with the seasons makes food exciting again. You'll only get to eat mangetout peas for maybe 3 months of the year – but what a 3 months they'll be. If you grow your own, you can feast on seasonal fresh food that you'd usually think of as luxuries. Eat asparagus with every meal for most of the spring

HOW TO EAT SEASONALLY

One good way to take a good long look at your eating habits is to keep a food diary. You

Globe artichokes are a true delicacy and one of the highlights of the summer garden.

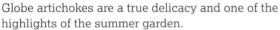

Get your key crops in place, and you'll know there'll be something to pick every month of the year.

don't need to be too pernickity about it – just a general list of the fruit, veg and herbs you've eaten in any given month will do. Use your list to gradually adjust your family menu, replacing out-of-season foods with similar but in-season ones. So, if you usually buy imported calabrese in February, get into the habit of buying more-locally-grown purple sprouting broccoli instead (it's actually much tastier too).

As an example, if you're living in the UK, what you can expect to be eating in your seasonal year goes something like this. From late autumn until mid spring, hearty brassicas like cabbages, sprouts and kale take the lead, plus those winter stalwarts, parsnips and leeks. Spring greens and purple sprouting broccoli are seasonal highlights which conveniently fill the 'hungry gap' too – that awkward spell in late spring where the harvest grinds to a halt unless you've planned and planted for it carefully.

Early summer is mouthwatering: it's asparagus time, and you can harvest the first over-wintered broad beans (fava beans), plus new potatoes and the earliest salads. High summer is a time of plenty: everything from beans and peas to courgettes (zucchini) and sweetcorn. From mid autumn the veg garden winds down, but you can still expect to harvest late crops of beans, plus autumnal crops like winter squash. Get these key crops in place, and you'll know there's something to pick every month of the year. And when you're picking year-round, you're halfway to being self-sufficient already.

Broad bean flowers and shoots are edible, as well as the actual beans and pods.

Some things will never be in season in cooler climates, of course: bananas, for example, or oranges. But we live in the twenty-first century, and it's a little perverse to banish them just because we can't grow them. A few bought-in oranges are a godsend in late winter, when there's nothing much else in the way of fruit around. So don't beat yourself up about it: just look forward to the day when you can stop eating boring old bananas and get back to feasting on garden soft fruit by the bucketload.

CHEATING THE SEASONS

The good news is that you can do your own out-of-season veg production too. Extend the core season of each fruit or vegetable, and you can pick several weeks earlier and for quite a bit longer than you would otherwise. There are lots of time-honoured tricks for extending the season:

❋ **Eat at different stages** Many seasonal delicacies are enjoyable for much longer if you free yourself from the straitjacket of only eating them one way. So snip curly-tendrilled mangetout pea shoots at about 10cm (4") long to enjoy raw in salads; eat garlic green in summer as well as dried at other times; and enjoy sprout tops in autumn, slicing off the cabbagey top growth whole.

❋ **Choose varieties carefully** Get to know your varieties, and you can manipulate the seasons by sowing a range that mature at different rates, to take over from each other through the season rather like a relay team.

Make two or three sowings of early peas like 'Meteor' through the season, for a long harvest.

For example, divide sowings of Brussels sprouts between the early-maturing 'Nelson' and late-maturing 'Revenge', and you extend your harvest from late autumn to early spring.

❋ **Stagger planting** Anything that takes less than a season to reach maturity, like French beans, peas, carrots, beetroot and chard, can be manipulated by sowing little and often, so you always have more growing while you're picking. Follow spring sowings with a second in early summer and again in high summer to crop into autumn, and you've got a season-long supply.

❋ **Use early warmth** Use heated propagators indoors or, outdoors, a clear polythene cloche (put in place 4 weeks earlier to warm the soil), and you trick seeds into germinating early. Cloches also keep crops such as parsley and cut-and-come-again

Set a heated propagator to about 18°C (64°F) to germinate most seeds.

Pot up a few strawberry runners in winter and bring them indoors for an earlier crop.

lettuce productive for longer at the season's end, protecting them from autumn gales and trapping the last of the summer's warmth.

✳ **Get a greenhouse** The sowing year in a polytunnel or greenhouse starts in late winter – with a correspondingly early summer harvest too. Average temperatures are routinely 3-5°C (5.4-9°F) higher under glass, so summer crops last well into late autumn, and your repertoire extends to hot-climate veg like aubergines (eggplant), chillies, sweet peppers, sweet potatoes and even watermelons.

✳ **Force plants** The ultimate out-of-season trick, forcing fools plants into growing much earlier by adding heat, or excluding light, so stems grow meltingly tender and sweet. Pale, delicate forced rhubarb stems are a welcome fruit hit in early spring: all you need to do is up-end a black dustbin over the dormant crowns in midwinter. Bring strawberries indoors after the first frost for berries a month earlier too.

You'll soon be coveting a polytunnel: this sumptuous example is at the National Trust's Knightshayes in Devon.

Build a hot box

For deluxe forcing, build a hot box in early spring: a 60cm (2')-deep pit filled with fresh manure, turned daily for a week beforehand to rev it up to stratospheric heat. Once it's cooled to around 20°C (68°F) — any hotter will scorch your plants — top with a layer of compost and sow with 'Paris Market' carrots, salads, peas and dwarf French beans for super-early crops.

SEASONAL TREAT GROWING GUIDES

There are some veg that simply define a season. Imagine a bowl of strawberries, and it's my guess you're also thinking sunshine, shorts and the soft thwock of tennis ball on racket. Brussels sprouts, and you're singing carols and warming your toes by the fire.

The veg featured in this section are my must-have seasonal highlights: the treats I look forward to all year. Start with two for each season, then expand your range from the table at the end of this chapter.

Spring

With light, melt-in-the-mouth flavours that are the essence of tender new growth, spring seasonal vegetables are about as sublime as it gets.

Asparagus

Lusciously tempting spears fat with delicate flavour, dripping with butter . . . asparagus is the taste of spring.

The appearance of the first asparagus shoots in spring is always a cause for celebration.

Season: Late spring / early summer.
Varieties: For an easy life, choose high-yielding modern varieties like 'Gijnlim'. Purple varieties like 'Pacific Purple' produce fewer but tastier spears.
How much to grow: About 20 crowns will feed a family of four generously.
How to grow: Buy 1-year-old crowns in spring, and plant in well-drained soil in a sunny spot. Make trenches 20-30cm (8-12") deep, heaping a 7.5cm (3") ridge of soil along the bottom. Sit crowns on top of this, about 35cm (14") apart, and back-fill with soil.
Care: Asparagus practically looks after itself. Your main jobs are weeding, keeping mulches topped up, and cutting yellowed stems back in autumn.
Pests and diseases: The one main enemy is the black-and-yellow asparagus beetle,

Purple sprouting broccoli is one of the delicacies of the early-spring veg garden.

its grey larvae an unpleasant find lurking in your asparagus spears. If stems suddenly turn to straw in summer, this is probably your culprit. Squash the larvae on sight, and bin or burn spent stalks to destroy overwintering adults.

Harvesting: Leave to grow for two seasons, till plants are producing fat, sturdy spears. Then slice the spears away at around 10-15cm (4-6") tall with a sharp knife, cutting about 2cm (1") below soil level (a curved asparagus knife makes the job easier). Stop cutting after about 8 weeks, to allow plants to recover.

Purple sprouting broccoli

Richer-flavoured than green calabrese (which is also – incorrectly – known as broccoli), I look forward all year to the PSB season.

Season: Winter to spring.

Varieties: There are early and late varieties of purple sprouting broccoli, so grow both to extend the season. 'Rudolph' is quickest to produce spears; add 'Early Purple Sprouting' and 'Late Purple Sprouting', and you'll be picking from late autumn to mid spring.

How much to grow: Once they get started, the plants are super-generous, so five or six plants will easily feed a family.

How to grow: Sow seed in early summer, one seed to a 2.5cm (1") module. Pot on into 10cm (4") pots, harden off in a cold frame and then plant out in a sunny spot, spacing 60cm (24") each way. Firm plants in well.

Care: PSB is pretty trouble-free as long as it's well protected against pests. It grows quite tall, topping out at about 90cm (3'), so in windier areas you need to stake the stems to prevent the roots loosening.

Pests and diseases: The many flying pests which adore brassicas — both feathered and six-legged — are kept at bay by growing the whole crop under a cage of fine insect-proof mesh. It won't keep slugs off, though, so patrol regularly and pick them off as you see them.

Harvesting: Pick the deep-purple florets as they appear, snapping them off cleanly from the stem at about 10cm (4") long. Keep picking regularly, as the more you pick, the more the plants produce.

Summer

Lazy, hazy summer: season of suntan cream and sand between your toes. Summer veg have flavours to match, each mouthful setting off little explosions of sweetness and delight.

Mangetout peas

Mangetout offers the essence of pea in a slender, crisp green package. Serve just steamed, with a little butter, and summer has arrived.

Season: All summer long.

Varieties: 'Oregon Sugar Pod' is a prolific flat-podded mangetout; 'Shiraz' has pretty purple pods and pink-and-violet flowers. The compact 'Reuzensuiker' is excellent in containers.

How much to grow: Two 3m (10') rows at peak production will let you feast for months.

How to grow: Sow five seeds to a 10cm (4") pot in spring. Once seedlings reach about 8cm (3") tall, harden off and plant the whole potful outside, without separating the plants, leaving about 15cm (6") between each group. Regular staggered sowings extend the harvest.

Care: Poke twiggy pea sticks into the ground among the seedlings, or string pea netting between canes for support. Tie in plants as they grow and keep them well watered, especially when they're flowering.

Pests and diseases: Mice find both the seeds and seedlings irresistible. Sowing into pots on shelving helps, or, if you're sowing direct, mulch with holly prunings. The only reliable mouse control, though, is a cat or a trap. Birds also peck at young pea shoots, though this is less common: if you have trouble, net the crop.

Harvesting: Snip pods away with scissors at 8-10cm (3-4") long, while still flat (for

Mangetout: essence of pea in a crisp, slender package.

flat-podded varieties) or just swollen (for sugar snaps). You can also let the pods swell into conventional peas: they're smaller and less flavoursome than proper podding peas, but still make good eating.

Strawberries

Dripping with sweetness, warm from the sun, just-picked strawbs are the essence of grow-your-own luxury.

Alpine strawberries drip with tiny fruits all summer and often well into autumn.

Season: Early-to-mid summer.
Varieties: 'Honeoye' is a good early fruiter; follow it with the vigorous 'Cambridge Favourite' and late-cropping 'Florence'. Perpetual ('everbearer') varieties like 'Mara des Bois' fruit sporadically till early autumn.
How much to grow: As much as you can manage – there's no such thing as too many strawberries!
How to grow: Buy bare-root runners in late autumn, and plant into a deep, rich, weed-free soil in full sun, spacing 35cm (14") apart, with the crown just at soil level. Or you can grow alpine strawberries from seed in spring. Strawberries are very happy in containers too: plant three to a 35cm pot.
Care: Keep plants well watered, and feed with a high-potassium liquid feed (tomato feed is fine) once flowers appear. As fruits form, tuck straw underneath to keep them clean. Trim off any long-stemmed runners regularly, and after cropping finishes shear off old leaves and mulch ready for next year.
Pests and diseases: A netting cloche keeps off birds (bury the edges to exclude mice too). Slugs are little terrors for strawberries, so keep your defences up (see Chapter 6, pages 124-5 for details).
Harvesting: Pull fruits away from the plants when they're absolutely red and ripe, snipping the stem to leave the tuft of leaves intact. Put the rest of your life on hold and enjoy as soon as possible.

Autumn

Treats are plentiful in autumn, as everything rushes to fruit before winter closes in – but my favourite autumn delicacies are aromatic and rich with colours to match the falling of the leaves.

Quinces

Fat, yellow, pear-like fruits with an ancient history, the quince is the model tree for a small garden. Naturally compact, low-maintenance and self-fertile, it never outgrows its space. With froths of shell-pink spring blossom and leaves that turn butter-yellow in autumn, quinces look gorgeous all year. And the huge crop of headily aromatic fruit is truly the scent of autumn.

Season: Early-to-mid autumn.
Varieties: 'Vranja' is a good all-rounder; the early-cropping 'Meech's Prolific' is scrumptious. Patio (dwarf) quinces make gorgeous container plants: 'Leskovac' (also sold as 'Serbian Gold') is among the best.
How much to grow: One tree is plenty: established quinces produce heavy crops.
How to plant: Dig a hole twice as wide as the rootball but the same depth (rest a cane across it and it should sit where the soil meets the trunk). Drive in a stake to cross the trunk at 45 degrees, backfill with soil, and firm the tree in before tying it to the stake and watering well.
Care: Water the tree well for the first two seasons. After that, quinces need little regular care: water in dry spells, and scatter slow-release fertilizer each spring, followed by a generous mulch.
Pests and diseases: Quinces are generally trouble-free, but watch for leaf blight in early summer. Blighted leaves turn blotchy and drop early. There's no cure: rake up affected leaves and burn them to prevent re-infection. If the fruits are holey, codling moth may be the culprit: use pheromone traps hung in the branches.
Harvesting: You'll smell when your quinces are ready: the heavy, sweet perfume can fill a whole garden. The fruits will still feel hard (they should be cooked before eating). Undamaged quinces store for up to 3 months.

Winter squash

Rich ochre squash, roasted in olive oil and rosemary, is bonfire food to warm you to your chilly autumn toes.

'Turk's Turban' squash are satisfyingly bizarre, and store for ages after harvest.

Season: Autumn to early winter.

Varieties: 'Butternut' is a good all-rounder, while 'Potimarron' (also sold as 'Uchiki Kuri') has a superb flavour, like sweet chestnuts. 'Hubbard' varieties keep the longest, sometimes up to a year.

How much to grow: One plant produces about six fruits. I reckon on three or four plants to feed my family.

How to grow: Sow seeds one to a 7cm (2¾") pot in mid spring and keep them frost-free. They grow rapidly into giant seedlings, so pot on as necessary. Once the threat of frost is past, harden off and plant out 1m (3'3") apart.

Care: Squash ramble around enthusiastically, throwing out huge weed-smothering leaves (they're brilliant ground cover under sweetcorn and climbing beans) without needing much encouragement: just redirect the occasional wayward shoot back on to the veg bed.

Pests and diseases: Slugs make short work of squash seedlings, so never sow direct. Plant out as vigorous youngsters, once they're able to cope with a little damage. Mildew can strike if plants are dry at the roots, so water thoroughly and pick off affected leaves promptly.

Harvesting: Let fruits ripen in the sun or indoors for a couple of weeks to 'cure' the skins for storing (see Chapter 1, page 32). Once ready, they'll feel hard and sound hollow when knocked. Store somewhere dry and frost-free.

Winter

I need a lot of sympathy and support in wintertime. And winter treats are just the way to do it: warming, filling comfort foods as consoling as a hearty hug.

Brussels sprouts

You ain't tasted sprouts till you've tasted home-grown. Crisp, tender, nutty – they're the perfect Christmas present.

Tasty and satisfyingly productive, Brussels sprouts are a must-have in the winter garden.

Season: Late autumn to early spring.

Varieties: 'Evesham Special' is ready long before anything else; follow it with the mid-season 'Trafalgar' for Christmas and 'Revenge' to take you through spring. The purple 'Rubine' has a seriously good nutty flavour.

How much to grow: Four or five plants each of three varieties will give you loads to pick.

How to grow: Sow one seed to a 5cm (2") module in early spring. Pot on seedlings as they grow, then harden off and plant outside in mid-to-late spring, about 75cm (30") apart.

Care: Sprouts don't need a lot of attention until they get really big – about 1m (3') tall in most cases. Sink a sturdy stake into the ground alongside each stem and tie plants in as they grow, to prevent gales blowing them over.

Pests and diseases: Grow under insect-proof mesh to fend off pigeons, cabbage white butterflies, aphids and whitefly too. Slugs like climbing the plants to chew holes in your sprouts, so you'll need good slug defences right through the season (see Chapter 6, pages 124-5).

Harvesting: Sprouts mature from the bottom up, so pick the lowest first, snapping them cleanly away from the stem. The 'sprout tops' (cabbagey top growth) are also delicious: slice them off just below the lowest leaves. Leave the stalk in the ground and the sprouts carry on developing as normal.

Parsnips

Earthy and humble, nothing compares to the sweet deliciousness of roast parsnips.

Season: Winter to early spring.

Varieties: Parsnips are much of a muchness, though 'Albion' and 'Palace' have good resistance to canker, and 'Avonresister' is short-rooted, so ideal for stonier soils.

How much to grow: Two 3m (10') rows gives you enough to harvest roots right through winter.

How to grow: Buy in fresh seed each year, as parsnip seed doesn't store well. Sow direct in free-draining soil from late spring. They'll take a while to come up, so be patient. Parsnip roots fork whenever they hit a stone, so if you have stony soil and want straight roots, either sieve the soil before you start, 'station sow' – make holes with a bar every 15cm (6"), fill with compost and sow a pinch of seeds on top – or grow in containers.

Care: Thin seedlings to 10-15cm (4-6") apart and keep weeded: and that's just about it. Parsnips are about as low-maintenance as they get.

Pests and diseases: Canker turns parsnip 'shoulders' to brown mush: avoid this by sowing later in spring and using resistant varieties.

Harvesting: Dig up roots at any time from early winter: frost helps sweeten the flavour. Parsnips can stay in the ground all winter, but older roots get quite woody, so lift some to store in boxes of damp sand.

WHAT'S IN SEASON WHEN

It can be hard to know what's at its best when, if you're not used to it – so this table outlines what you can expect to be eating fresh at any given time of year. Some crops are available all year round: long-season stalwarts you can always grow somewhere on the plot. Others are special treats, available for one season only – so grab them while you can! And then there are the veg you can eat from store, out of season, for that nostalgic taste of summer in the depths of winter. Storing and preserving your surplus produce is covered in Chapter 9.

The table is intended as a guide rather than a precise calendar, and the exact timings for each harvest will vary, depending on whereabouts you are, and of course on the weather. The timings shown here are for an average UK season: for cooler climes, expect to start picking a few weeks later and finish slightly earlier; if you're in a warmer location, you'll start a few weeks earlier.

	Winter		Spring		Summer		Autumn	
Apples								
Artichokes, globe					■			
Artichokes, Jerusalem	■							■
Asparagus				■				
Aubergines (eggplant)					■	■		
Beans, broad (fava)								
Beans, French								
Beans, runner								
Beetroot								
Blackberries								
Blackcurrants								
Blueberries								
Cabbage	■							
Calabrese					■			
Carrots								
Cauliflower			■					
Celeriac	■							
Chard	■							
Cherries					■			
Chillies								

	Winter		Spring		Summer		Autumn	
Courgettes (zucchini)							Marrows	
Cucumbers								
Garlic			Green garlic					
Gooseberries								
Greengages								
Kale								
Kohlrabi								
Leeks								
Onions								
Parsnips								
Pears								
Peas				Mangetout				
Plums								
Potatoes				New				
Pumpkins								
Purple sprouting broccoli								
Raspberries								
Redcurrants								
Rhubarb		Forced						
Salad leaves								
Spring greens								
Sprouts								
Squash								
Strawberries								
Swedes								
Tomatoes								
Turnips								
Whitecurrants								

Key

Seasonal treats that can't be stored.

Seasonal treats, but storable, so you can still enjoy them out of season.

Long-season stalwarts.

Healthy plants and plentiful harvests come easily when the growing is good.

Chapter Six

THE GOOD GROWING GUIDE

> *"Use all the tricks of the trade to nurture your crops, and you'll reap generous rewards."*

The main thing to remember about plants is that they really, *really* want to grow. So, mostly, if you sow a seed it will come up; and if you put a plant into the soil it will produce roots, a stem, some leaves and probably at some point a flower.

As a vegetable grower, though, particularly one trying to feed yourself from the plants you're tending, it's in your interests to help them grow as well as possible. You want them to produce not just leaves, but loads of leaves; not just flowers, but a positive waterfall of blooms, leading to generous basketfuls of fruit – and that includes tomatoes, courgettes (zucchini), beans and peas – for you to eat.

Encouraging your plants to flourish is what good gardening is all about. So this chapter is all about the little tricks and strategies you can use to help your plants not just grow, but thrive.

Rich soil equals plentiful crops and delicious platefuls at mealtimes.

Defining beds saves time and concentrates all the goodness in the soil around your plants, where it's needed.

EARTHY MATTERS

When you want to grow good veg, start from the bottom and work your way up. The brown stuff in which your plants have their roots is your most precious resource, and is also a small miracle of evolution and ecology: one single teaspoonful of soil contains about a billion microorganisms, most of which we can't even name yet. Nearly all of them have a function in helping your plants grow. Once your soil is as close to perfect as you can make it, the rest will follow.

So look after your soil and you'll nourish your plants. Support nutrient levels by 'feeding' the soil with organic matter (well-rotted farmyard manure or home-made compost are ideal), packed with minerals including nitrogen, potassium and phosphorus – the building blocks for healthy plants. Look after the delicate balance of your soil's ecosystem: that same organic matter will open up clay soils and bind together lighter sand and chalk. Evict nutrient-sapping weeds and root-forking stones as you go, and eventually you'll reach soil nirvana: a loose, friable loam, the texture of crumble topping and the colour of dark chocolate, in which plants can reach triffid-like proportions. It's a gradual process and you'll need to keep at it too, but you'll be rewarded with crops that grow sturdier, faster and more productively from year to year.

The key to nurturing your soil is to **mulch, mulch, mulch**: keep any bare soil covered with organic matter at all times, to lock in moisture and suppress annual weeds. Pile on that manure, compost, even grass clippings (used sparingly, as they do heat up) and shredded cardboard: anything that will rot down and feed your soil. The worms gradually pull organic matter into the soil, improving its structure and feeding your plants for you. Ground-covering plants like squash do much the same job simply by covering the ground with their leaves, although they don't feed the soil in the way that adding organic matter does. So where you're not growing plants, mulch.

Get to know your soil

There are three main types of soil, although most soils fall somewhere between these extremes.

❋ **Clay soil** is sticky and easily rolls into a sausage. It is easily compacted but nutrient-rich: stay off it in winter, and add organic matter to break apart those sticky clods.
❋ **Sandy soil** falls apart easily. It is easy to work in bad weather but 'hungry' – nutrient-poor – so needs continually topping up with organic matter. Sandy soils also need more watering.
❋ **Chalky soil** is crumbly and greyish. It is easy to work but shallow: build up the topsoil with organic matter. Chalky soil is also alkaline, which brassicas love but potatoes don't.

Clear perennial weeds

Perennial weeds are the bad boys of the veg plot: rampant thugs which quickly swamp, strangle or out-compete your carefully tended vegetables. They come back year after year –

> *How to grow*
> *straight carrots*
>
> When growing carrots in stony soils, drive a crowbar into the ground and wiggle it about to make a deep hole. Fill with a 50:50 mix of compost and sand, and sow into the top for long, straight roots.

bigger each time if you let them – and most are capable of regenerating from the tiniest of roots left in the soil. Keep on top of them right from the start, and you'll keep them at bay. Heck, if you're determined enough you may even (after some years) get rid of them altogether.

❋ **Dig out as much as possible.** Nettles and brambles come out well, but bindweed, couch grass, ground elder and mare's tail go deep and regenerate easily – so it's more realistic to aim to control them in the longer term rather than to dig out every last bit.
❋ **Keep your soil covered** with black polythene or thick cardboard whenever beds are empty, especially in winter.
❋ **Hoe weekly** throughout the season. Even perennial weeds can't survive having their heads constantly chopped off.

To dig . . . or not to dig?

Digging used to be a given on veg plots: you'd see blokes in flat caps trudging out to the allotment, trusty spade in hand, to double-dig the whole thing from top to bottom. That's digging to twice a spade's depth and tipping organic matter deep into the soil – very hard on the back, not to mention the soil!

This thinking is now largely discredited: the soil's ecosystem is a delicate balance of billions of microorganisms, fungi and soil particles, and slamming a spade into it does it no favours at all. So keep digging to a minimum and your soil stays intact, ready to support your plants.

❋ **Dig once** to get some organic matter into poor soils for a good crop in your first year. After that, leave well alone, to develop a good ecosystem fed by mulches on the soil's surface.

❋ **Never dig in winter,** as you'll compact the soil into a lifeless pan of rain-sodden mud. Instead, mulch thickly with compost and cover with black polythene to keep the soil dry and weed-free till spring.

Making garden compost

Try to find space for a compost bin or three, as they're invaluable for returning nutrients to the soil.

To make good garden compost, aim for a 50:50 mix of 'browns' – slow-to-decompose materials such as ripped-up cardboard, straw and animal bedding – and nitrogen-rich, fast-decomposing 'greens', including kitchen waste, grass clippings, animal manure and green leafy plant material.

Turn compost regularly –at least every 6 months, but more often will break it down quicker. Cover it and keep it damp, and within a year you should have lovely black, crumbly compost ready to spread on your soil.

Making compost is an essential skill to master, turning greenery into brownery that has a magic effect on your soil.

LOOKING AFTER BABY

Most plants in a vegetable garden are raised from seed: it's an economic way to produce the quantities of plants you need to give yourself a decent-sized harvest. You can't cut corners when raising from seed. Use good-quality compost and seed, then simply cater for your little ones' every need. Master the art of germinating seeds and raising healthy, strong seedlings, and you're off to the best possible start.

You don't have to sow from seed, of course: ready-grown bought-in 'plug plants' are often more convenient, especially for plants you'll only need a few of, such as squash or Brussels sprouts. But it's not very self-reliant: so whenever you can, save your own seed and use it to raise next year's food (more on seed-saving in Chapter 8).

Baby plants are at their most vulnerable.

Don't cut corners when raising plants from seed: use good-quality compost and the freshest seed.

Start with the right materials

The raw ingredients are so important to get right. Care taken now will always pay off later on, in big, healthy seedlings that turn into generously productive plants.

※ **Seed compost:** Use good-quality, fresh seed compost. You can make your own from leafmould, sand and garden compost (see Chapter 12, pages 212-13 for details). At first, though, until you've built up your home-made compost supplies, it's easier to buy it instead (see box on page 123).

※ **Seed:** Use seed that's as fresh as possible – home-saved is freshest of all! Never use seed over 2 years old, and always fresh seed for parsnips and carrots.

※ **Water:** Many seed-killing diseases live in rainwater, so use bug-free tap water instead.

Sow direct or under cover?

It's a dilemma. Do you start your seeds off indoors on a windowsill or in a propagator or greenhouse, sowing them carefully in pots or module trays – with all the extra watering and potting on into larger containers that that involves? Or can you afford to just sow them direct into the ground? The truth is that sometimes it's fine to sow direct – while other times you'll get better results if you sow under cover, where it's warmer and safer and you can keep a closer eye on your babies.

Sow direct:

❄ when soil temperatures rise above 10°C (50°F) – day and night

❄ when sowing hardy, cool-climate seeds like carrots, beetroot and spinach

❄ when sowing plants which don't like being transplanted, like coriander.

Sow under cover:

❄ early in the season, while it's still cold at night

A greenhouse bench is ideal for raising seedlings, but a table in a sunny room indoors does fine too.

❄ where slugs are a problem

❄ when sowing tender, hot-climate plants like tomatoes, squash or peppers.

Common problems with seedlings

Baby plants are so tiny that any setback is major. So stay on your guard, and act fast if you see signs of trouble. Here are the main things to look out for.

Slug damage

Symptoms: Seedlings are eaten to the ground: look for tell-tale slimy trails.
Prevention: Raise seedlings under cover and plant out as more resilient youngsters.
Cure: Wildlife-friendly ferrous phosphate slug pellets, or see pages 124-5 for other methods.

Greedy birds

Symptoms: Leaves look ripped in half; seedlings may be torn out of the ground.
Prevention: Net seedlings from the outset, burying or pegging down the edges securely.
Cure: As long as the damage is only to leaves, plants should recover.

Damping off

Symptoms: Soil-borne fungi infect entire trays of seedlings, which then collapse overnight, sometimes in circular patches.
Prevention: Sow sparsely, so air can circulate among the seeds; don't overwater.
Cure: Watering with a copper fungicide often helps fend off the worst effects.

Pot on seedlings regularly as they grow.

A cold frame is a useful bit of kit when you're moving seedlings around.

Leggy seedlings

Symptoms: Seedlings grow weak and spindly, sometimes with pale, sickly leaves.
Prevention: Lack of light is the culprit: put off sowing till a little later in the season.
Cure: Use grow lights or move seedlings to a brighter spot.

Flea beetle

Symptoms: Tiny shot holes in leaves of young brassica seedlings.
Prevention: Grow seedlings under insect-proof mesh from the start.
Cure: Pass honey-smeared cardboard over leaves: beetles leap up and get stuck.

Hardening off

For seedlings raised under cover, the open garden is a shock. Adapting takes time, so they need to be 'hardened off' slowly and gradually.

How to do it: Take about 10 days to 2 weeks to expose seedlings to outdoor conditions. Move them into a cold frame to act as a kind of half-way house between a greenhouse and the open garden. Open the lids in the mornings, then all day, and finally on mild nights too.

Watch out for: Cold snaps are quite common at the time of year when you're hardening off seedlings. Cover cold frames with bubble wrap, or just move your trays of seedlings back indoors until things improve.

Sowing in dry weather

If you're sowing direct when the weather is dry, really soak the bottom of the drill before sowing, so the seed is in contact with damp soil from the start. This will improve germination.

Veg-growing jargon-buster

Sometimes it can seem like those in the know are talking a whole different language when it comes to veg-growing. Here's an explanation of a few terms you may hear bandied around.

Allium: Anything in the onion family, including shallots, leeks and garlic, as well as onions.

Brassica: All things cabbagey: includes sprouts, kale, broccoli and cauliflower, plus (of course) cabbage.

Cloche (row cover): A low glass or plastic tunnel which fits over a row of plants and protects them from the weather. Invaluable for protecting vulnerable plants and extending the season at both ends.

Cold frame: Basically a large box with windows instead of a lid. It sits on the ground and acts like a mini greenhouse to keep seedlings sheltered on their way out into the open garden.

Crop rotation: The practice of moving crops in the same family (e.g. legumes, brassicas or roots) around the plot each season to prevent pests and diseases getting hold.

Earthing up: Pulling earth up around stems to protect them from frost (potatoes), blanch them (leeks) or encourage more roots to form up the stem (tomatoes and potatoes).

Legume: Anything in the pea and bean family: generally they improve a soil's nutrition, as they can 'fix' (draw down into the soil) nitrogen from the air.

Modules: Seed tray inserts divided into individual compartments, usually about 5cm (2") square. Seedlings grow into little 'plug plants' to plant out as they are; no pricking out required.

Nutrients: The minerals and other essentials your plants extract from soil to keep themselves healthy, like vitamins in food. Nitrogen, phosphorus and potassium are the main ones.

Organic matter: Anything that used to be a plant – so garden compost, cardboard, vegetable peelings and rotted farmyard manure are all organic matter.

Perennial weeds: Weeds which come back year after year, like bindweed, mare's tail, ground elder and couch grass. (In contrast, annual weeds grow, set seed and die in one season.)

Cold frames get very busy in spring.

pH: Acidity or alkalinity, which is important where soil is concerned. A pH of more than 7 means alkaline soil, which brassicas will love; a pH of less than 7 means acid soil, great for peas and potatoes. Most soils are neutral, with a pH of 7.

Pinching out: The practice of removing the growing tip (the topmost shoot) from a plant to encourage bushiness (in young plants) or to stop upward growth so fruit can ripen (in tomatoes and cucumbers).

Plug plants: Seedlings with a small root-ball ready to be potted on before going out in the garden, with no need to break or otherwise disturb their roots.

Potting on: Moving a plant up into a slightly bigger pot to give its roots fresh compost to grow into.

Pricking out: Breaking apart seedlings, usually when they've developed two or three pairs of leaves and are big enough to handle, and moving them into their own individual pots to grow on.

Propagator: A seed tray with a clear cover to intensify sunlight, warm the compost and encourage seeds to germinate quicker. Heated propagators have a heating element in the base too.

Transplanting (planting out): Moving a young pot-raised plant out into its final growing place in the garden. You can also transplant self-sown seedlings into a better growing spot.

A consistent water supply is the key to vigorous, healthy crops and bumper harvests.

WATERY WISDOM

Every child knows that when you plant something, you have to water it to get it to grow. But this most basic gardening chore is actually one of the most difficult to get right. Ideally, you're aiming to keep your plants' water supply as constant as possible; in practice, it's a balancing act between meeting their needs while minimizing the amount of time you spend lugging watering cans around.

What and when to water

You can't water all your plants the same: drought-lovers may need none at all, while thirsty triffids need pints every day. If it's sunny – especially if there's a brisk breeze – plants are wilting before you've refilled the watering can; on a cool, cloudy day, overwater them and they'll drown. So watering is a bit of a tactical game, requiring delicate calculations and the weighing of multiple options before finally making your move.

What to water:

* Just-sown seeds and emerging seedlings.
* Youngsters that you've just transplanted outside.
* Leafy plants like spinach and rocket, which are prone to bolting if dry.
* Flowering plants – you'll boost your harvest.
* Plants in containers and under cover.
* Plants under cloches and in cold frames.

What not to water:

* Tomatoes that are fruiting: too much watering makes for insipid tomatoes.

* Drought-lovers like Mediterranean herbs and onions.

When to water

Water early in the day in spring and autumn, so plants don't sit in the wet through a cold night. The moisture then soaks in while the morning warms up, getting to the root zone before the sun gets too hot. But switch to watering in the evenings through the height of the summer, when even the morning sun can be warm enough to evaporate water

Water only the plants that really need it, like these just-planted courgettes.

away, to give plants all night to absorb the moisture instead.

That said, if something is clearly gasping for water, don't wait till the 'right' time – water it!

Checking for dryness

You can't tell if plants need water just by looking. Soil that appears dry can be sopping wet underneath, while just after a rain shower the earth looks wet but is often bone dry just an inch down. Just to confuse things further, plants can wilt when they're overwatered too. So carry out some checks:

* Lift pots to see how heavy they are: well-watered containers are heavy, so if it feels light, it's dried out.
* Stick your finger in the soil: if it doesn't feel damp to the touch right down to your fingertip, water it.
* Dig with a trowel and you'll see from the colour of the soil how far down the damp-ness goes: the paler the soil, the drier it is.

Water-saving strategies

There comes a time in almost every summer – even the dull ones – when the rain just stops. A few preventive measures, plus some nifty tricks borrowed from hot-climate gardeners, keep plants from going thirsty.

* Install drip irrigation to deliver water right by the roots where the plant needs it. These come as individual 'drippers' to insert in the soil, or just as leaky hosepipes ('soaker hoses') to lay on, or just underneath, the soil, where they ooze moisture

Use a Spanish trick: instead of watering the whole bed, make irrigation channels between rows of crops.

steadily over time. Attach the system to a tap or water butt pump, and use a timer or just turn it on yourself for as long as needed.
* Cut the bottom off a 2-litre (4-US-pint) plastic drinks bottle, remove the lid and sink it upside-down alongside your plants. Fill the bottle to deliver moisture direct to the roots.
* Make a little moat around thirsty plants like squash, and the water collects in it instead of running away across parched soil, holding it in place to soak right in.
* Instead of watering the whole veg bed, use a Spanish trick and make shallow irrigation channels between your rows of crops. Fill the channels, and the water is delivered to the roots either side.
* Mulch continuously to prevent moisture evaporating – but make sure you only mulch over damp soil, as mulching dry soil traps the dryness too.
* Use low-growing ground-cover plants such

Nasturtiums make a fantastic – and decorative – ground cover, locking moisture into the soil.

as squash, melons, nasturtiums or red clover to scramble about under taller plants, shading the soil and helping to prevent evaporation.

HEALTHY DIETS

Soil nutrients are as necessary for good plant growth as food is for animals: if they go short, you'll find that malnutrition sets in, in the form of yellowing leaves, stunted growth and poor harvests. Feeding isn't always necessary – especially if you have good soil – but carefully targeted injections of fertilizer at certain times in the growing year can improve health, encourage growth and, best of all, boost production.

What to feed and when

Mostly, plants don't need any more food than they get from good soil, stuffed to bursting with organic matter and treated with care so it delivers all the moisture and nutrients a plant could need.

But some soils need special care to correct imbalances. Chalk, for example, prevents plants absorbing iron and manganese, while acid soils dissolve away trace nutrients like calcium and copper. And plants in containers depend on you completely. Most veg gardeners have to feed their plants at some point: get to know how, when and what, and you'll really boost your results.

Plants to feed:
* Plants in containers.
* Flowering plants.
* Plants in greenhouses.
* Plants which are ailing – for example after a pest attack.
* Leafy crops like spinach and salads.

Plants not to feed:
* Herbs – they prefer poor soils.
* Seedlings – you can 'scorch' seedlings with too much feed.
* Plants at the end of the season – that sappy, overfed growth is also more vulnerable to frost.

What kind of fertilizer

Fertilizers divide into two main kinds: slow-release, and fast-acting liquid fertilizers for instant results.

Slow-release fertilizers deliver nutrients over a number of months. These include pelleted poultry manure; bonemeal; and blood, fish and bone. Scatter twice a year, in spring and in early summer.

Liquid (quick-acting) fertilizers major on different types of nutrient. I switch between liquid seaweed for general-purpose feeding, nitrogen-rich home-made nettle tea for leafy growth, and high-potassium tomato feed or home-made comfrey tea for anything flowering

or fruiting. See Chapter 12, page 209 for how to make your own liquid feeds.

A year-round feeding regime

Follow this annual routine, combining slow-acting organic fertilizers, to inject goodness into the soil all season long, with occasional pick-me-ups where needed, and you won't go far wrong.

Early spring:
* Work slow-release fertilizer into veg beds prior to planting out.
* Scatter slow-release fertilizer around established fruit bushes and trees.
* Give spring cabbages and other over-wintered veg a boost with liquid seaweed.

Mid spring:
* Feed leafy crops like spinach and mixed salads with high-nitrogen nettle tea.
* Six weeks after planting up containers, start feeding weekly with liquid seaweed.

Early summer:
* Top up slow-release fertilizers to see crops through to autumn.
* Continue feeding leafy crops with high-nitrogen feed once a week.
* Give asparagus beds a slow-release fertilizer after you stop harvesting.

High summer:
* Feed tomatoes, cucumbers and peppers with high-potassium tomato feed.
* Give a high-potassium feed to flowering peas and beans too.
* Watch out for plants looking stressed as a result of insect attack, and feed them to boost growth.

Late summer / early autumn:

✳ Stop feeding now, so plants can die down naturally for winter.

Common mineral deficiencies

Like people, plants need a good balance of 'vitamins' – minerals which occur naturally in the soil – to stay healthy. Once they start going short of these, they look decidedly sick, but quick diagnosis followed by a shot of fast-acting fertilizer soon puts things right.

Nitrogen

When it appears: In spring, in plants grown on unprotected soil after winter rains leach nitrogen away; and at any time of the year in container-grown plants which have used up the limited supply of nutrients in the compost.
Symptoms: Pale-yellow leaves; spindly growth.
Cure: Scattering pelleted poultry manure at the start of the season and stepping up

Get expert growing help and advice

Join a gardening organization like the Royal Horticultural Society (RHS) in the UK, or the American Horticultural Society (AHS) in the USA, to get member services such as disease diagnosis and soil analysis.

mulches of organic matter helps avoid this happening in the first place, but if you need a fast-acting fix, go for a foliar feed (sprayed directly on the leaves) of liquid seaweed or a drench with diluted nitrogen-rich nettle tea.

Potassium

When it appears: Common on light sandy or chalky soils, where potassium is easily washed out.
Symptoms: Yellow or purple leaves, browned at the edges; poor flowering and/or fruiting.
Cure: Apply liquid tomato feed or home-made comfrey tea in the watering can as a drench.

Magnesium

When it appears: Most often caused by over-use of potassium-rich fertilizers like tomato feed.
Symptoms: Characteristic yellowing between the green leaf veins.
Cure: Spray diluted Epsom salts on foliage fortnightly, and fork them into the soil as well.

Iron

When it appears: Common on acid-loving plants like blueberries planted in soil with too high a pH (too alkaline).
Symptoms: Yellowing between the leaf veins and a failure to thrive.
Cure: Apply chelated iron to the soil, mulch with composted bracken or pine needles – or, better, move the plant to a more acid environment, such as a pot containing ericaceous compost.

Use the right compost

Different potting composts are formulated for different uses, so make sure you choose the one that's right for your needs. You'll find compost sold under two main formulations: seed compost and multipurpose (there are specialist composts too, such as ericaceous compost for acid-loving plants like blueberries). Most ordinary composts are made of a mix of organic materials, like composted green waste and bark; in contrast, soil-based composts contain a high proportion of topsoil. They're more expensive, but many gardeners swear by them, as they hold on to nutrients for longer. You can also make your own potting compost, varying the ingredients and proportions for the different formulations (see Chapter 12, pages 212-13).

If you are buying your compost in, do go for the best quality you can afford, with a trusted brand name (ask gardening friends for recommendations if you're not sure). There's a lot of cheap, badly made compost out there, but you pay for the saving in disappointing results and sickly plants: it really isn't worth it.

Seed compost is low-nutrient and sterile (disease-free), to give tender seedlings a good start without overfeeding them.

Multipurpose compost contains about 6 weeks' worth of nutrients and is ideal as an in-between compost for potting-on seedlings before they are transplanted outdoors (it's also fine for using in containers, though once the nutrients run out you'll have to start feeding).

Soil-based composts (often found as 'John Innes' formulations, named for the soil scientist who came up with the recipes) are heavier but hold on to their nutrients for longer. Just to confuse matters, these also come in lots of different types: so you'll find John Innes seed compost and John Innes No. 1 (for potting on seedlings), No. 2 (great for veg containers) and No. 3 (ideal for long-term planting in containers, as with fruit trees and bushes). Mix John Innes composts half-and-half with potting composts, and you get a good halfway house that works for most container plants.

Don't overfill pots: always leave an inch or so below the rim for watering.

KNOWING YOUR ENEMIES

Unfortunately, you're not the only one who enjoys your veg. There are legions of insects, birds and mammals out there intent on feasting on the food you've so thoughtfully grown for them – to say nothing of the hosts of fungal organisms who'd like to set up home on the plants' leaves, stems and fruits. Good gardening requires a degree of mild paranoia. You'll be one step ahead of your enemies only if you're perpetually on your guard. Follow the 'PEA' principles below and you'll keep most trouble at bay.

* **Prevention:** Barriers, good garden hygiene, disease-resistant plants and healthy crops all stop the little beggars getting near your crops in the first place, and no pests means no problem.
* **Early signs:** Patrol regularly, concentrating on leaf undersides, young shoot tips and

Know what you're dealing with

Make sure you've got the right diagnosis: for example, red spider mites turn leaves yellow between the veins, just like magnesium deficiency. Be sure you've ruled out everything else before deciding on the true culprit.

leaf joints, and looking for the first smidgin of trouble. And as soon as you spot anything, move on to . . .
* **Action:** Squishing a few aphids as soon as you see them is far easier than reversing the damage caused by established infestations. So do something straight away before they can take hold.

Rogues' gallery: common pests and diseases

You will come across some garden baddies more often than others. The following are your prime suspects – starting with those most likely to be the culprits in your veg patch.

Slugs and snails

Found on: Most plants, though some (tomatoes, for example) are less prone to damage.
Prevention: Minimize hiding places and restrict access to your plants: replace grass paths with hard landscaping, and sow any

Caterpillars are particularly partial to cabbages, with an appetite that grows as fast as they do.

Second only to slugs in the gardener's list of wildlife you love to hate . . .

vulnerable plants like lettuces under cover, up on shelves, where slugs can't find them.

Early signs: Seedlings razed to the ground; on older plants, leaves with irregular holes. Slime trails are the giveaway clue.

Action: Use several methods: regular slug hunts, wildlife-friendly ferrous phosphate slug pellets, 'slug pubs' made of yoghurt pots sunk into the ground to their necks and half-filled with beer or milk (the slugs love beer and crawl in to meet a boozy end) – all make inroads into your local populations. The water-on nematode *Phasmarhabditis hermaphrodita* (a lethal parasite of the slug) is also very effective in beds of vulnerable crops, like lettuce.

Caterpillars

Found on: Brassicas and nasturtiums.

Prevention: Grow under insect-proof mesh from the start.

Early signs: Holes in leaves, with whole plants eventually reduced to stalks. This is easy to mistake for slug damage, so look closely at leaves to spot caterpillars at work.

Action: Pick off caterpillars every day, plus any yellow egg clusters, to get things under control.

Aphids

Found on: All sorts of crops, and each different kind of aphid (there are many) has its preferences. So you'll find greenfly on greenhouse crops and fruit trees, blackfly on beans, and mealy cabbage aphids on brassicas: they may look quite different, but they're the same underneath, and equally as damaging.

Prevention: Grow under insect-proof mesh; pinch out broad bean tips in early summer to thwart blackfly, and clean greenhouses in autumn to prevent aphids overwintering inside.

Early signs: Look for yellowing, distorted shoot tips and 'sooty mould' – actually a secondary infection growing on the honeydew the aphids secrete.

Action: Squish small colonies of aphids between finger and thumb. For larger infestations, spray with insecticidal soap.

Vine weevils

Found on: Container-grown plants, and occasionally outdoor strawberries.
Prevention: Wrap pots in insect-proof mesh or fleece; destroy adult weevils on sight.
Early signs: Otherwise healthy container plants wilt, then keel over, with C-shaped grubs clearly visible in the compost.
Action: Tip plants out of pots, pick out grubs, wash roots under the tap and re-pot in fresh compost.

Larger pests

Found on: Almost all plants grown in the open ground.
Prevention: Fencing with 1.2m (4') chicken wire is the only sure way to keep out larger mammals like rabbits: bury the bottom 30cm (1') in the ground, and add a couple of strands of wire on top to deter deer.
Early signs: Rabbits nibble the tops off mature plants; and rabbits, squirrels and deer chew the bark off fruit trees. Badgers and foxes tend to uproot plants, while rats and mice strip corn cobs and eat just-planted bean seeds.
Action: There are some plants rabbits and deer don't like – onions, rhubarb and cherries, for example – but if you want a full range of veg, keep them off the plot. Trap rats and mice – or keep a feral cat.

Late blight

Found on: Potatoes and tomatoes.
Prevention: Blight-resistant varieties are your only sure defence. The 'Sarpo' potato range is excellent; blight-resistant tomatoes include 'Ferline', 'Losetto' and 'Mountain Magic'.
Early signs: Late in the season, often after a spell of wet, warm weather, brown blotches appear on the leaves. Plants collapse, and death is only a matter of time.
Action: Damage limitation is all you can hope for. Cut away potato haulms (stems) and you should save the tubers becoming infected, and trim away tomato leaves as they turn brown, to slow the spread.

Mildew

Found on: Courgettes, cucumbers and melons are all very prone, as are grapes.
Prevention: Keep susceptible plants well watered and growing on strongly towards the end of the season, and thin leaves so air can circulate more freely around the plant.
Early signs: A powdery grey dusting appears on leaves, spreading rapidly to affect all the leaves on a plant. Usually appears in autumn, when roots are dry but the air is damp.
Action: Pick off affected leaves promptly and you'll slow the spread. Dispose of infected leaves in the bin or the bonfire, as mildews can survive winter on old foliage.

Rust

Found on: Onions, leeks and garlic; also apples, mint and gooseberries.
Prevention: Grow alliums 'hard', without feeding, as excessive nitrogen makes for soft, sappy growth that's fair game for rust infection.
Early signs: Dusty copper-orange powder appearing on green leaves, which rapidly yellow.
Action: Picking off affected leaves slows the

spread of the fungus, but once plants are infected they are hard to cure. Dispose of infected plants carefully, as the rust fungus survives composting.

Clubroot

Found on: Brassicas, including mustard, radishes and swedes.
Prevention: Lime more acidic soils, as clubroot dislikes alkaline conditions. Grow resistant varieties like the cabbage 'Kilaxy', and raise seedlings to a good size before planting them out.
Early signs: Plants fail to thrive, becoming stunted and poor; leaves take on a purple tinge. When you pull up the plant, the roots are swollen and distorted into fat, twisted knots.
Action: Clubroot is dreaded by veg growers, as it persists in the soil for 7 years or more, so once you've got it, you've got it for good. If possible, avoid growing brassicas in known infected areas.

Viruses

Found on: Most veg, but especially strawberries, rhubarb, cucumbers and tomatoes.
Prevention: Aphids are known carriers of viruses, so keep on top of infestations. Look out for virus-resistant varieties and only buy plants from certified virus-free stock.
Early signs: Distorted growth; leaves which develop streaks, speckles and splashes; and odd-shaped fruit are all symptoms.
Action: There is no cure, so dig up the plant and destroy it. Never propagate from a plant known to have suffered from a virus.

Cultural problems

Many 'diseases' are actually caused by less-than-perfect growing conditions. Here are some of the avoidable problems you might come across.

✳ **Blossom end rot:** Black, corky lesions on tomatoes are caused by erratic watering. Aim for a constant level of moisture in the soil, watering more on sunny days and less when it's cloudy.

✳ **Etiolation:** When seeds grow long and lanky, leaning towards the light, they make weaker plants. Sow later in the year, when light levels are better, and if raising seedlings on windowsills, turn plants regularly.

✳ **Bolting:** When plants run to seed early, it's a sign of stress – if they go thirsty too long, for example, or if they overheat. So keep leafy crops like spinach and rocket well watered and grow them in shade to keep them damp, and avoid overcrowding.

✳ **Failure to set fruit:** Lack of pollinators often leads to poor fruiting: so leave greenhouse doors and windows open to give pollinating insects access, and hand-pollinate (using a soft artist's brush) early in the season.

Part Two

DIGGING DEEPER

With an allotment you can garden even in the middle of a city: this plot is an energetic stone's throw from the City of London

Chapter Seven

FIND MORE SPACE

"You don't need to own land to find more growing space: from neglected gardens to community schemes, there's plenty of land in need of more growers."

The only problem with this self-sufficiency malarkey is that it's a bit addictive. The first rule of growing veg is that however much space you have, it will be around 25 per cent less than you actually need. Once you've got the taste for salads snipped straight on to the plate, sun-warmed strawberries and peas so sweet you eat them raw, a potful or two isn't quite enough any more. You start hankering after a proper crop of potatoes, perhaps, and a big generous asparagus bed. An orchard would be nice . . . Once you start daydreaming like this, the inevitable has happened: you need more growing space.

The good news is that you don't need to own any land to expand your horizons: just borrow some. In this chapter I'll be exploring the ways you can get your hands on the dozens of neglected gardens and abandoned patches of no-man's land out there just begging for attention. I'll explain the difference between the various kinds of communal schemes, from allotments to community gardens to full-on farms. Collective growing schemes are springing up everywhere – a fantastic way to learn from fellow gardeners, meet a whole new bunch of people and take home proper arm-filling quantities of home-grown food. Just get out there and take a look around you: there's more land available than you may think.

Garden sharing is a great way to pool resources.

GARDEN SHARING

You'd be amazed how many people have a garden but can't look after it. Look around your neighbourhood and you'll find singletons too busy on the office commute to spare time for the weeding, or senior citizens who simply aren't as mobile as they once were.

This is where you come in. Match a keen gardener who's short of a garden with a garden owner who's short of time, energy or ability, and it's a tailor-made fit. In return for a share of the produce, you get enough land for those self-sufficiency dreams (and, who knows, a new friend into the bargain).

You can arrange garden shares informally: ask a neighbour you know is struggling, put an ad in the local shop, or just put the word out. If your town is part of the Transition Towns movement, you'll find that garden-sharing schemes are often part of the package – sometimes backed up by training for gardeners who are just starting out. And charities are getting in on the act too: Age UK, for example, uses garden-share schemes as one way to help older people stay in their own homes.

Increasingly, matching services are available online too. In the UK, schemes like Lend and Tend, Glasgow Land Share, or the Facebook group Landshare include ads from large-scale landowners to private householders. There's a similar site in France, Prêter son Jardin. In the USA, Urban Garden Share started in Seattle but now includes cities from California to Georgia, while Shared Earth – originally based in Austin, Texas – now connects gardening

Ten questions to answer for a good garden share

Sort out a few ground rules between you and the garden owner before you start, so you both know where you stand. You'll avoid all sorts of silly disagreements later if you establish the answers to these questions now.

✳ How much time can you commit?
✳ Does the garden owner want to get involved in planning, or will you have a free hand?
✳ Are there any restrictions on your gardening activities? Some garden owners are happy for you to plant permanent features like fruit trees, for example, while others are not.
✳ When will it be possible to access the garden – and how?
✳ Where should you park your bike or car? How far is it to public transport?
✳ How are you going to divide up the harvest? Just by helping yourself, or by percentage?
✳ Do you bring your own tools or is the garden owner happy for you to use their wheelbarrows, hoses, etc.?
✳ Who is responsible for expenses such as seed, compost, fertilizer, materials for raised beds and repairs to sheds and fences?
✳ What about utilities: who pays the bills for water and electricity use?
✳ If the owner won't be there when you visit, how will you communicate? It's important to establish a good system of communication – whether by phone, email, text messages or written notes. A regular face-to-face meeting (once a month, say) is a good idea. Regular communication is key to avoiding misunderstandings.

Garden sharing is a great way to match growers with garden owners – and you might make some lifelong friends.

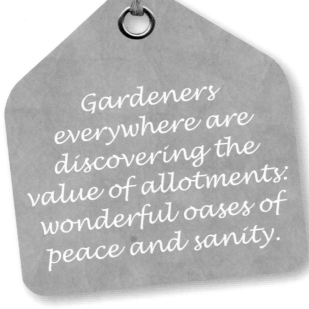

Gardeners everywhere are discovering the value of allotments: wonderful oases of peace and sanity.

people with gardens across America. Sharing Back Yards operates a similar scheme throughout Canada. For links to further information on garden sharing in different countries, see the Resources section.

Like any agreement, sharing a garden needs a careful approach to make sure it works for both parties and stands the test of time. Discuss openly what you both want from the arrangement and, if possible, draw up a written contract, so you have the foundations in place for what should be a long and happy partnership.

ALLOTMENTS

A more traditional route to getting your hands on some growing land without actually owning any is to rent an allotment: a slice of land owned by the local council and leased

(usually very cheaply) to anyone who wants to grow their own food. When I acquired my first allotment, these sites were rather forgotten places, generally occupied by a few old-timers pottering about at the end of a hoe. How times have changed. Nowadays, frustrated gardeners everywhere are discovering the value of these wonderful oases of sanity, peace and fresh food.

When the Smallholdings and Allotments Act was passed in the UK in 1908, obliging councils to provide allotments, the size of a plot was determined as the amount of land considered necessary to feed a family of four. That works out as 10 rods (the traditional measurement), or 250m^2 (300 sq yds): about 21m x 10.5m (70' x 35'). They were right too: my allotment was easily enough land to keep our family in beans, rhubarb, beetroot and strawberries (plus much, much more) all year round. So this is a useful benchmark if you're wondering how big your vegetable garden needs to be. However, most modern allotments, under pressure from encroaching development and increasing demand, are half the traditional size.

The right of the common man to get his hands on a patch of land to grow food stretches back at least as far as medieval times. In Great Somerford, Wiltshire, Britain's oldest allotments are still going strong on a 2.4-hectare (6-acre) site first set aside for the benefit of 'the labouring poor' by request to George III in 1809. Allotment land is a Europe-wide tradition, and is now making inroads in the USA too, where many community gardens have started to rent plots of land to individuals (see page 138).

Allotment plots are wonderful little parallel universes, where the cares of the world slip away and all that matters is good food and good company.

Key questions to ask when taking on an allotment

When you're offered the keys to your first allotment, it's easy to get swept away with the excitement of it all – but rein it in for a minute or two and ask yourself a few crucial questions to make sure you know what you're letting yourself in for.

✳ Where's the water supply? A tap should be within reasonable hose-pipe reach – it's rarely possible to save enough rainwater to keep you going year-round.

✳ What state is it in? You'll probably have to do some clearance work, as allotments are often left in quite a neglected state by their previous occupants. Some councils will help you clear it if it's really bad.

✳ How shady is it? Big trees and tall buildings cast such deep shade that it's difficult to grow anything underneath. Try to find a plot that's in sun for as much of the day as possible.

✳ What are the rules? All allotment sites have a rule book: check first to find out whether you're allowed to put up sheds and greenhouses, plant fruit trees or keep small-scale livestock like chickens or bees.

✳ What weeds will you have to tackle? Even brambles can be defeated with persistence, but large clumps of Japanese knotweed, giant hogweed or mare's tail should make you pause and probably say no.

✳ How easily can you get there? You'll want to visit your allotment often, so the closer it is, the better. If you're on a bike or public transport, invest in a secure shed so you don't have to cart heavy tools back and forth.

Check your plot out thoroughly before you start.

There are loads of different models in different countries. Danish allotment holders have pavilions on their allotments and are allowed to live there all summer. Not all allotment holders pay rent: in Germany, the 5 million *Schrebergärten* holders buy their plots for a peppercorn sum, but there's a condition enshrined by law that they are only to be used as gardens. In the Soviet era, the *dacha* (a simple country retreat with a garden) was the only land freely available to individual working people: though most of those in Russia are now privately owned, their legacy is still going strong in the fiercely defended allotment sites of Poland, the Czech Republic and Latvia.

Unfortunately, getting your hands on a plot isn't always straightforward. Waiting times can stretch into years: the longest in the UK is an eye-watering 40 years for residents of Camden Borough in London, although that is an extreme example! But it's still worth putting your name down: often, by the time people get to the top of the list they've lost interest or their circumstances have changed, so the waiting list can move faster than you'd expect.

You might also be able to start up your own allotment site, if you know of a disused patch of public land. And allotment sites are increasingly leased not only by councils but also by private individuals and companies. Look out for information at work: thanks to enterprising employees pestering them for lunch-break gardening opportunities, there are now workplace gardens and allotments on-site at companies from the BBC to shoemakers Timberland and, in the USA, wholesale grocers C&S.

Gardening with other people gives you on-tap advice and a sympathetic ear for your triumphs and disasters.

More information can be found from the National Allotment Society (UK), the European Federation of Allotments and Leisure Gardens, and the American Community Gardening Association: see Resources for details.

COMMUNITY GARDENS

When you're gardening on borrowed land, it soon becomes more than 'just' gardening. Share a garden, and you forge a close link with its owner; take on an allotment, and your allotment neighbours quickly become as familiar to you as your house neighbours (more familiar in many cases). Gardening alongside other people gives you on-tap advice and a sympathetic ear for your triumphs and disasters. It's community gardening at its very best.

Perhaps that's why so many people are signing up to volunteer at organized community gardens, in which large groups of people come together to jointly raise food for themselves. If

A well-run community garden is a friendly and sociable way to learn the ropes.

you're not too confident about your abilities as a veg grower, it's an excellent way to learn the ropes.

Community gardens operate on many different models. In the USA, the term 'community garden' is often used to mean 'allotment' – but there's also a growing number of hybrid schemes, offering some plots for private use but with a large communal central area, closer to what Europeans mean by community gardens. There's a strong tradition of urban community gardens in the USA: New York's Green Guerillas are perhaps the best-known community garden activists, reclaiming the most unpromising scraps of urban wasteland for communities to grow food on, from Brooklyn to the Bronx.

In Canada too there's been a huge surge in the popularity of community gardens, as news spreads of their benefits to health and communities. A community garden on the roof of McGill University in Montreal helps to feed older people in the local area as well as its gardeners; and in Edmonton, the gardeners include Ukrainians, Poles and Koreans, who regularly get together to hold what must be one of the most multicultural home-grown pot-luck dinners in the world.

Giving surplus produce to the local community is a common theme in community gardening. Grace & Flavour, a community garden in a walled garden leased from the National Trust in Surrey, UK, donates a fixed share of the produce to homeless charities, hospices or retirement homes in the local area. Volunteer gardeners can buy back the veg they help to grow at a fraction of the shop cost.

Many community gardens also have an educational and social side, running workshops or giving gardening spaces to schools or people with mental or physical disabilities. Others are mixed economies: the 1.4-hectare (3½-acre) Mastin Moor Community Gardens in Chesterfield is a mixture of small individual growing spaces, community plots, wildflower meadows and orchards.

Before you commit to being involved, make sure you're happy with the terms and conditions and are really clear about what you're getting yourself into. Visit the garden several times – most community gardens have open days or are willing to show you around.

It's not an option for control freaks either! Most community gardens are run by committee, with everyone having a say in what's grown, so you may not always get to grow exactly what you want. But community gardens are a really easy way to get growing – most are short of volunteers and welcome newcomers gladly. You'll get your hands in the dirt much sooner than if you sign up on an allotment waiting list too; in fact, many people volunteer at the local community garden while waiting for an allotment plot to come up.

Find out more from the umbrella organization for community gardens in your country – the snappily titled Federation of City Farms and Community Gardens (FCFCG) in the UK, or the American Community Gardening Association in the USA and Canada. They'll be able to tell you all about how community gardens work, and also point you towards a community garden near you.

So if you enjoy meeting other gardeners and like a gossip while you're weeding; if you value the reassurance of always having someone on hand to ask when you're not sure – then community gardening could be the option for you. Plus the cake and coffee is really good.

COMMUNITY SUPPORTED AGRICULTURE

Take your community gardening to the max at a Community Supported Agriculture (CSA) farm, and you can add eggs, lamb, beef, pork and maybe even honey to the list of food you're producing yourself. A growing number

Goats, sheep, cows, geese and bees live alongside the gardeners at the Surrey Docks City Farm in central London.

Most CSA schemes offer a mixed economy, with communal growing areas alongside livestock.

of farmers are tapping into the army of willing volunteers out there who are prepared to shoulder the cost and the burden of looking after land and animals in return for a share of the produce. And – this being farming rather than gardening – the produce includes meat and eggs too.

Many CSA farms are similar to community gardens, with added chickens, cows, sheep and pigs (and in some cases goats, geese, ducks and bees). It's a great way to get into livestock-keeping without needing to know it all before you start – and crucially, without having the tie and commitment of keeping stock animals yourself. You also get to add home-produced food that you might really struggle to provide at home: things like cheese and milk, which really need farm-sized amounts of land and specialized equipment if you're to produce the sort of quantities you need for self-sufficiency.

While the name is American, the seed for the CSA movement was sown in 1950s Europe, where the increasing industrialization of food production was beginning to ring alarm bells. As time went on, concern grew: it became increasingly apparent that the burden of responsibility for producing food for the vast majority of the population was falling on the shoulders of the tiny minority who happened to earn a living as farmers. The CSA model shares the load more evenly, linking farmers more closely to the communities they serve and reconnecting people to the land that feeds them. It's a determined turn away from globalization and towards a local and sustainable model of food production. Plus you get to scratch a sheep behind the ears at weekends.

CSAs work as a kind of shareholding arrangement between farmers, who own and manage the land, and the community around them, which benefits from the food they produce. Most operate on a partnership model between farmer and volunteers, but the type of land ownership varies. In the UK, Chagfood in Devon rents 2.4 hectares (6 acres) of land on a 3-year rolling farm tenancy to grow their 50 varieties of vegetables to supply a veg box scheme, plus an orchard of apples and other fruit trees. Oak Tree Low Carbon Farm, inspired by the Transition Towns movement in Suffolk, is owned by a market gardener who works in partnership with the community team. On their 4.8-hectare (12-acre) smallholding they keep chickens, cattle and rare-breed pigs, as well as growing vegetables, some on a permaculture system.

Anyone can take part: you buy shares, with the capital raised used towards the farm's running costs, and in return you also share what the farm produces. The great thing about CSAs is that, because they are community-driven, you get much more of a say in how they're run: most are organic, and at Chagfood they even have two horses taking the strain instead of less-sustainable tractors.

You can choose different types of membership: in some CSAs you buy more expensive 'produce only' shares, while in others you can opt for 'working' shares – offering a reduced subscription price in return for a few hours a week mucking in alongside the farmer. And some CSAs 'pay' their volunteers in produce – so the more work you do, the more food you take home with you.

Contact your local umbrella organization to find out more: in the UK, the FCFCG (see page 139) can put you in touch with city farms, or for other CSA schemes try the CSA Network UK. In Europe, Urgenci links CSAs across the continent (and some further afield), while in the USA, LocalHarvest acts as a hub for CSA schemes with listings for CSAs around the country. See the Resources section for details.

The range of livestock kept on CSAs is often much wider than you'd manage at home.

Peas and beans are among the easiest veg for seed-saving.

Chapter Eight

SAVE YOUR OWN SEED

> "*All plants want to reproduce, and some types of seed are ridiculously easy to collect. By saving seed, you complete the self-sufficiency circle.*"

Buying seed from a seed merchant each year to raise your own food is the equivalent of shopping for cardboard boxes in order to recycle them. All the veg in your garden have a vested interest in reproducing. Help them, and you get next year's supply of fruit and veg for free. Save your own seed and you close the self-sufficiency circle, creating a kind of perpetual motion food supply for as long as you're around to grow it.

Before there were seed merchants, everyone saved their own. Particularly valued varieties were passed on to family members or swapped with the neighbours: many old favourites, such as 'Crystal Apple' cucumbers, 'Alderman' peas and 'Brandywine' tomatoes, found their way into seed catalogues and are still prized today. But these days we've largely lost the habit of seed-saving: it's too easy to reach out for a seed

Don't be too quick to deadhead annuals like marigolds: leave a few flowers to set seed for next year's crop.

straightforward given a basic knowledge of botany and the possession of some horticultural fleece. We'll start with the easiest seeds – peas and beans – then get a little more adventurous and add annual herbs, tomatoes and a host of other crops to the list of seeds you don't have to buy any more. You'll never look back.

SEED-SAVING TECHNIQUES

Seed-saving starts when the plant is in its prime, as that's when you single out specimens that are particularly big, vigorous and healthy, or have other qualities you want to preserve.

packet from the shelves instead of bothering to collect your own.

I don't pretend that I've collected every single seed I sow: I'm just not that organized. But beans, peas and tomato seeds are so easy to save that it seems ridiculous to spend money on the packeted version instead. And once you've started, it's hard to stop. After you've mastered the beans, you can't resist letting the purple sprouting broccoli bolt, just to see if the seeds come true (they do). Soon there are elastic bands on the pumpkin flowers and flowering parsnips in the garden, and you're waxing lyrical on winnowing techniques.

In this chapter I'll show you how to save seed from pretty much every kind of vegetable you grow in your garden. I'll also demystify apparently technical stuff like hand-pollination and isolation cages – which are actually perfectly

Collecting seeds as they ripen, for sowing next year, is part of the harvest if you want to be self-sufficient.

Grow your own heritage variety

When a plant grows in the same garden for generations, each successive branch of its family is genetically that bit better adapted to thrive in your microclimate of soil type, water levels and local weather conditions. Save seed from the one survivor of an outbreak of disease, and its offspring have a genetic ability to resist that pathogen in future.

Start experimenting with the plants now growing in your garden, or buy in varieties you particularly want to grow and save their seed for future seasons. Just avoid F1 varieties (they'll be clearly marked as such on the packet), as they won't come true from seed.

By the time you've been doing this for a few years, you're growing plants which are well suited to and do especially well in your garden, with a gratifying harvest to match. In short, you're developing

Grow the same plant year on year for generations – these are climbing borlotti beans – and they'll be perfectly adapted to conditions in your garden.

your own heritage variety to share with the gardener next door, your children and perhaps your children's children, one day.

Mark the plant (or fruit) you want to save seed from with a piece of coloured wool knotted around the stem, so you remember not to pick it for eating. It may seem counter-intuitive not to harvest your best plants, but it's essential if you want to continually improve your stock. If you save seed from the dregs left over at the end of the season rather than selecting in this way, you'll end up with weak, spindly plants –

plus you're effectively selecting plants which fruit late, which means their offspring will be predisposed to delay their own harvest too. Sometimes, of course, that's a quality you want – the best leafy veg, for example, are those which flower latest. But you'll still want to choose the leafiest, biggest, heftiest specimens for seed, as they're the ones that will pass on good genes to their offspring.

Mark your best plants with a piece of coloured wool so you remember not to eat your seed bank.

Store saved seed in paper envelopes and keep it somewhere cool and dark.

Collect your seed during a spell of dry weather, when you can be sure that seed pods are at their most crisp. Timing is important: leave your peas too long, for example, and they burst open and shed the seed by themselves. If you're worried, either tie a paper bag over the ripening seedhead or err on the early side and cut the whole plant to hang upside down and finish drying indoors, with a sheet underneath to catch any errant seed.

Clean the chaff from seed as much as possible, but don't stress about it too much: there is some evidence that seed stays viable for longer when stored with its chaff. Just make sure it stays dry, as debris can make your seeds more prone to mildew.

Finally, always remember to label your seeds with the name and date: they should last at least 2 years from the day you collect them; sometimes more if stored well. But when you have an ample supply each year, there's no reason not to sow fresh each season, thereby guaranteeing the highest possible levels of germination.

Have a go at saving the easiest seed first: mainly pods – beans and peas – which just pop out of their packets clean and ready to store. Once you've got the hang of it, try annual flowers or lettuces – which are also straightforward but need a little clean-up before you put them away for the winter. Build up your seed-saving confidence gradually, saving from something a little different and more ambitious each year, until you're piling up premium seed stocks for every vegetable in your garden.

Wait till pods are dry and crispy brown before harvesting the seeds.

Pods

Use for: Broad beans (fava beans), runner beans, French beans, peas (including mangetout and sugar snap), rocket.

Podding vegetables have the easiest seeds to collect, as all you have to do is wait for them to dry on the plant, then shuck out the seeds to store.

Peas are largely self-pollinating, so will come true to type – that is, the offspring will be identical to the parents, so you can rely on getting the same variety characteristics again.

French beans are mostly self-pollinating, but are occasionally visited by pollinating insects, so, to be sure, grow just one variety and to plant them at least 1.8m (6') away from other people's crops.

Other climbing beans, including runner beans and borlotti beans, will cross-pollinate: isolate plants if possible (see box on page 155), or get your neighbours to grow the same variety as you! Rocket does cross-pollinate, but since it's a species (i.e. close to a wild plant) rather than a cultivated variety, it will come back true to type anyway.

Allow the pods to mature on the plant. If it's wet, collect them as they start to yellow, and lay them out somewhere dry for about a week until they're brittle (most pods rattle when shaken at this stage). Take the seeds out and dry them for a few more days out of their pods: they should be dry enough to break when you bite into them. Store them in a paper envelope, ideally inside a sealed container in the fridge.

Annual herbs

Use for: Coriander (cilantro), chervil, dill.

Annual plants germinate, flower and set seed in the same year. They're designed to self-seed copiously, and if you leave them to their own devices you can usually find little clusters of seedlings around the base of the spent plant, which you can then carefully dig up to transplant to where you want them to grow – bypassing the whole seed-saving thing altogether. For a bit more control, though, collect seed at the end of the plant's life, to store and then sow direct in spring. This is essential for non-hardy herbs like coriander, whose seedlings won't survive a harsh winter.

Coriander, dill and chervil produce their large, easy-to-handle seeds in sprays, or umbels, which are straightforward to collect. Save seed from the plants which are last to set seed – i.e. slowest to bolt – as that means future generations will stay leafier for longer too.

Let them dry on the plant if possible, but be careful, as they can drop their seeds when your back is turned. Check them every day: as soon as the seeds are starting to come loose, they're ready. If it's wet, just wait till they're starting to turn brown, then cut the whole head (umbel) and bring it indoors to dry on a sheet of newspaper. When the seed is fully brown, rub it off the heads with your fingers and discard the stems. Pick out any debris and store the seed in a paper envelope.

Save seed from the coriander plants that are last to start flowering.

Lettuce and flowers

Use for: Lettuce, basil, pot marigolds (*Calendula officinalis*), nasturtiums.

Lettuces are self-pollinating, so you don't have to worry about keeping the seed pure. They are also prolific and will happily self-seed all over your plot if you let them. For quality crops, though, save seed from your best specimens: those with exceptional size, texture and flavour – and which are also slowest to bolt.

Lettuce heads ripen bit by bit: either harvest the seed as it ripens or (less time-consuming) wait till most of it's turned brown and dry and then cut the whole head at once. Up-end it into a bucket, then shake the ripe seed off into the bucket. The seeds will come away

Lettuce plants send up massive flower spikes and produce copious amounts of seed.

with loads of chaff, so put the lot in an ordinary kitchen sieve and shake gently. Some seeds will fall through; others settle to the bottom of the sieve. Pick as much chaff as possible off the top, and store the seeds more-or-less clean (you don't have to be too particular) in a paper envelope.

Basil seed is collected in much the same way: let a flower spike ripen, then cut it and rub off the seeds to store. It will cross-pollinate, so grow just one variety if you don't want to end up with a cross between different varieties.

Pot marigolds and nasturtiums have large, easy-to-handle seeds, which are a cinch to collect. After the flowers drop, the seeds generally dry naturally on the plant. The curved marigold seeds turn a nutty brown and come away easily from the heads when fully ripe. Nasturtium seeds, which look like baby chick peas, are ready to store as soon as they drop off the head easily (just give the head a light tap).

Umbellifers

Use for: Carrots, parsnips, parsley.

Lots of the vegetables we grow as annuals are in fact biennials, producing leaves and roots in the first year, then flowering and setting seed the year after. Of these, the umbellifers are by far the largest group: their close family connection is quite obvious when you look closely, as all have thick, pointed tap roots and huge, showy, dinner-plate-shaped flower heads.

The other trait they share is their ability to cross-pollinate, and they easily revert to their tougher, spindlier wild relatives if you're not careful. Parsley is the easiest to save seed from, as there are few varieties, although flat- and curly-leaved varieties will hybridize, so stick to one or the other.

For root veg like carrots and parsnips, keeping seed true to type isn't usually a problem,

Leave a parsnip in the ground into summer, and it will produce a towering flower spike.

as so few gardeners let their biennial veg run to seed – so it's unlikely there will be another variety flowering nearby. However, carrots will cross with Queen Anne's lace (wild carrot / *Daucus carota* subsp. *carota*): this is almost impossible to prevent, so be prepared for a few white, spindly roots among your future carrot crops.

Leave the crop in the ground over winter, then in early summer it will send up a 1.5m (5')-tall flower topped with a gorgeous flat umbel of flowers. Once these go over and dry into sprays of brown seeds, cut the whole thing and up-end it into a brown paper bag. Shake or rub the seeds off the head, remove any chaff, and allow it to dry further for a few more days before storing in a paper envelope.

Maintaining genetic diversity

Saving seed from just one plant each year is the vegetable equivalent of inbreeding for insect-pollinated crops. A limited gene pool is likely to result in spindly plants and poor-quality harvests within just a few generations.

So keep your crops' gene pool well stocked by letting several plants or even an entire row run to seed, saving a few seed from several of the best plants to sow the following year.

The more plants you let run to seed, the better the genetic diversity: aim for at least half a dozen specimens for larger plants like brassicas, and up to 40 for smaller plants like carrots. Of course, this isn't always practical, but just do the best you can. If you grow on an allotment, you could always pool resources: each gardener takes turns producing seed for a season while everyone else grows a harvested crop to share or barter for the seed.

Beets

Use for: Beetroot, chard, perpetual spinach (leaf beet).

Beets are biennials, so leave plants in the ground all winter and they'll flower the following year. If you're saving beetroot and can't tell which root it's best to keep, you can dig them up to select and then replant your prize specimens to grow on.

All types of beet are terribly promiscuous – and because they're wind-pollinated, too, they'll cross-pollinate with every other beet for miles. Beetroot will cross-pollinate with chard and perpetual spinach, so you must isolate beet plants if you want to save their seed. Choose six to eight plants growing close together and drive a stake into the ground next to them. Then, as the flower heads form, tie them together around the stake and cover the whole thing with a bag of fleece. Shake this from time to time to distribute the pollen.

Harvest the brown, prickly seed as soon as it's dry, cutting away entire flower heads and up-ending them into a bucket before rubbing off the seeds. They're quite large, so are easy to pick out of the debris. Dry them for a little longer before storing in a paper envelope.

Alliums

Use for: Leeks, onions.

Alliums are another promiscuous group of biennials, needing careful handling to keep a variety true to type. Onions don't cross with leeks, but do hybridize with shallots, while leeks will cross-pollinate with elephant garlic.

All the allium family (leeks, onions, shallots and garlic) produce drumstick balls of ivory-white flowers in their second year.

Keep varieties pure by allowing only one variety to flower. If your neighbours' onions are also flowering, build a fleece isolation cage around your plants (see box on page 155) and hand-pollinate daily by brushing each flower in turn with a soft artist's brush. Once you see black seeds within the flower head, put a paper bag over it, up-end it and cut it off to finish drying indoors. It's then easy to shake or rub the seeds out of the heads for storing.

The pretty yellow flowers of all brassicas (this is pak choi) are delicious to eat – but leave some to set seed!

Don't be tempted to save seed from bolting onions that send up a flower spike in their first season – they're actually flowering a whole year early: since they're biennials, they shouldn't flower until their second year. Any offspring of these early bolters will also flower early, which spoils the bulbs. Just lift your crop as usual at the end of the season, and select five or six of the best bulbs to save seed from next year. Dry these just like the rest of your crop and set them aside. The following spring, plant them out again, burying the base of the bulb to 5cm (2") or so, and they'll send up a tall ivory-white flower spike.

Leave leeks in situ, and they'll also send up a spherical spike of flowers in their second summer, which you can save in the same way.

Brassicas

Use for: Cabbages, calabrese, broccoli, Brussels sprouts, kale.

Big, brash brassicas are among my favourite candidates for seed-saving, partly because the lush emerging flower spikes are delicious to eat. But I leave one or two to flower and make huge sprays of clattering pods – easy to crack open and collect the seeds inside.

Brassicas are closely related, so they do cross-pollinate: your Brussels sprouts can hybridize with kale; your cabbages with calabrese. That's great if you're experimenting, but not so great if you want to grow Brussels sprouts, or kale, or cabbages next year. Insect-proof isolation cages are no good here, either, as brassicas need insects to travel between plants to do the pollinating.

So limit yourself to saving just one type of brassica seed in any year. Dried and stored well, they should keep for around 2 years, so you can do your seed-saving in rotation: kale this year; calabrese next year, perhaps.

Once ripe, brassica seed pods shatter easily, so don't wait too long before you harvest your seed. Once most of the pods look dry, cut the whole flowering head and bring it indoors to hang over a sheet, where it will continue to ripen for a few days. Then crush the pods and use a kitchen sieve to separate out the little black bullet-like seeds.

Potatoes

Use for: All potatoes (early, second-early and maincrop).

Take no notice of the dire warnings to the contrary: it's perfectly possible to save your own seed potatoes to grow again next year. Like so much else, we've just fallen out of the habit of doing so. As long as you rotate your crop each year and have soil that's in good heart, saved tubers from last year's crop are as likely to thrive as bought-in seed stock.

The golden rule, however, is never, ever to save tubers from diseased plants. So if you've had an outbreak of blight this year, you're stuck with buying fresh seed potatoes next spring. Otherwise, it's a straightforward process.

Choose your best plants to dig up, then pick out undamaged tubers a little smaller than a hen's egg. Brush off excess soil, then leave

Spuds for tea – with a side order of seed potatoes for next year's crop too.

Leave home-saved seed potatoes on a windowsill for a few days to turn green.

When saving seed, allow fruiting vegetables to ripen as much as possible.

them on a bright windowsill for a few days to turn green – this triggers dormancy, so they won't sprout through the winter. Then pop them into egg boxes and store somewhere dry, dark and frost-free, with good air circulation. Plant them out as usual in mid spring.

This method should keep you in seed potatoes for several years, especially if you only select from large, healthy plants. Your only risk is from viruses, which are unusual in a home vegetable plot, but might be able to build up in untreated saved seed potatoes. If you notice that your whole crop is becoming spindly and disappointing, don't mess about: stop saving seed from that strain and start again with certified virus-free stock from a reputable seed merchant.

Fruiting vegetables

Use for: Tomatoes, chillies, peppers, aubergines (eggplant).

Most plants with fleshy fruits, from tomatoes and peppers to aubergines, are found in the greenhouse. That makes them super-easy to isolate – and a good thing too. Although modern tomatoes are self-pollinating, older varieties, including potato-leaved and currant types, are not. Aubergines hybridize readily with each other, and chillies and sweet peppers also cross quite happily. Stick to one variety when saving seed, or make an isolation tent (see box on next page) inside the greenhouse.

Leave fruit on the plant until it's so ripe it's almost dropping off, then separate the seed from the flesh. Chillies and sweet peppers are easiest: slice the fruit in half and scrape out the seed. Dry for a week before storing.

You'll find lots of conflicting advice about saving tomato seed, but my method has never failed me yet. Take a very ripe tomato, cut it in half and scoop out the flesh on to a piece of kitchen towel. Spread it around so the seeds are evenly spaced, and leave to dry on a windowsill. Pop the towel – seeds and all – into a paper envelope, then next spring simply lay it on the surface of a seed tray filled with compost, cover with a little more compost and wait. You should have seedlings in a couple of weeks.

Cut aubergines into quarters lengthways, put them into a bowl of tepid water and work the seeds out with your fingers. Good seed will sink to the bottom; the debris and bad seed should float. Spread them on a sheet of kitchen towel and leave to dry, then you can pick them off or just save the whole paper towel as with tomatoes.

Cucurbits

Use for: Pumpkins, squash (summer and winter), cucumbers, melons.

Sadly, saving the seed from your Hallowe'en pumpkin is never a good idea. We did that once and ended up with a big ugly lumpen yellow squash – a sort of squmpkin, we decided. It certainly wasn't going to make any lanterns for the doorstep.

To stop squash, pumpkins, courgettes (zucchini) and gourds cross-pollinating you'll have to do it yourself. Identify male and female flower buds (male with a straight stalk; female with a swelling fruit behind) when they're turning yellow and about to open, and secure them shut with a rubber band. Next day, take off a male flower, remove the petals and undo one of the female flowers. Dab the male flower into the female, then close up the female flower again. Tie a piece of coloured wool around it so you know which fruit you're saving.

When you harvest that fruit, scoop out the seeds and spread on a piece of kitchen towel to dry on the windowsill. Then pick off the seeds to store in a paper envelope.

Build an isolation cage

Isolation cages keep pollinating insects – and, more importantly, the 'foreign' pollen they may be carrying – off your flowers. Group four or five plants under an isolation cage, and they will only be pollinated by each other.

The principle is the same outdoors or indoors. Sink four canes into the ground at each corner of your group of plants. Then connect horizontal canes across the top, binding them together with twine to make a box about 20cm (8") clear of the plants.

Cover the whole thing with insect-proof mesh, then bury the bottom about 5cm (2") into the soil or weight it down securely with bricks, so nothing can get underneath.

You can hand-pollinate melons and cucumbers too: to keep pollinating insects out, grow the plants under fleece (more feasible than with the larger cucurbits!). Then dab a soft artist's paintbrush into the middle of each flower in turn, weekly for about a month. Let cucumbers ripen far beyond when you'd eat them – they should turn dark yellow. Scoop out melon seeds as for pumpkins; filter out cucumber seeds as for aubergines, letting the good seeds float to the bottom of a bowl of water before scooping them out to dry.

Home-made preserves are just one of the joys of growing your own.

Chapter Nine

PRESERVE YOUR PRODUCE

"From freezing and drying to making jams, chutneys and pickles . . . get clever and creative to make the most of your garden's abundance."

At some point in your veg gardening career – probably about 6 months after starting, in fact – you'll face a produce mountain. You'll be the lucky owner of the mother of all piles of courgettes (zucchini), or apples, or runner beans, in the kind of quantities the population of a small town would struggle to get through.

No matter how carefully you time your successional sowings and calibrate your quantities to deliver optimum supplies at precisely even intervals, there are some kinds of veg that just won't be told and insist on delivering their payload all at once. Courgettes are notorious for it: you spend weeks waiting for the first fruits, then they turn up and within a month your picking rate has hit three a day and you're feverishly scanning recipe books and wondering whether the kids would eat courgette ice cream.

Storing surplus produce quiets your inner Ukrainian: come the apocalypse, at least you know you'll never go short of canned apricots.

Make your own recipe book

Keep a folder of favourite glut recipes – to turn veg that don't store well, like courgettes and aubergines, into ready meals that you can pull from the freezer as you need them.

And in any case, there comes a point in the season where a bountiful autumn tips into the beginnings of winter, and if you don't get all your produce in right now, the first frost will arrive and that lovely veg will be lost to brown mush.

This is when I channel my inner Ukrainian. Like Ludmilla in Marina Lewycka's wonderful book *A Short History of Tractors in Ukrainian*, I am driven by some deep, instinctive urge to load my shelves to groaning each autumn with pickles, jams, canned fruits and preserves. I even had to buy a second freezer in case the apocalypse arrived and caught us short of a 6-month supply of runner beans.

But though friends and family might laugh, it's actually just good self-sufficiency. Eke out your summer harvest for as long as possible, and your winter crops go further too. Preserving enables you to keep yourself fed from your garden for more of the year than would otherwise be possible.

This chapter is all about tucking away your harvest, squirrel-like, so you get to taste summer-grown beans in the depths of winter and hardly notice the lack of fresh fruit as you pull stored apples from the shed and defrost punnet after punnet of blackberries (not to mention dipping into pots of home-made jam). Plus I'll give you the low-down on long-term preserving, from pickles and chutneys to canned fruit and jam, so you can enjoy every last mouthful of abundance your garden can offer.

STORING THE SURPLUS

Best of all is summer produce preserved as closely as possible to the way it was when you picked it, giving maximum versatility and an experience almost as good as eating it fresh. Many vegetables and fruit can be stored with little or no processing – so can be used in your cooking in the depths of winter just as you would if you'd picked it from the garden.

In general, the vegetables that store best are those that grow slowly and those with firm skins: like winter squash, which take all season to mature; or plump little peas and broad beans. Thin-skinned produce like lettuce, courgettes and cucumbers don't keep well and collapse into mush on freezing, so your best option is to cook them into dishes first.

Maincrop (late-maturing) varieties take the longest to mature, so have the most staying power in storage. Grow an extra bed or potful of maincrop carrots, peas or potatoes alongside your summer harvest just to lay down for winter, and you'll be able to enjoy them for months after the last fresh one is a distant memory.

Drying

Use for: Chilli peppers (except the fleshier types, like 'Rocoto Red'), pumpkins, winter squash, onions, softneck garlic, shallots, shelling beans (e.g. kidney beans, borlotti beans, cannellini beans), apples, pears, plums, some herbs.

Good drying is all about taking your time and choosing the right spot. The best-ever drying place I had was an unheated corridor between two back doors. It was cool and bright but out of direct sunshine, and there was a constant breeze as people walked through. I hung chillies, herbs and lavender from the walls, and they were perfectly dried within a fortnight.

Plait dried onions into a string and hang them in the kitchen for that rustic farmhouse look.

Outdoor drying, on the other hand, is all about curing the skins to harden them into a carapace which preserves the food within. It takes about 2 weeks: ripen pumpkins and squash on the plant, lifting them on bricks so the air can circulate and dry the skins fully. When ready, they'll sound hollow when knocked. Dig up your entire harvest of onions, shallots and garlic once the foliage turns yellow, to lay on the soil's surface. If the weather is damp, bring everything indoors (into a greenhouse if you have one), and continue the drying under cover.

Freezing

Use for: Berry fruit, climbing (pole) beans (e.g. French beans), broad beans, peas, fresh herbs, chilli peppers (fleshier types), spinach, perpetual spinach (leaf beet).

I prefer freezing to drying, as I find that flavours stay closer to fresh – especially in the case of herbs, whose essential oils are fragile and easily lost by drying, but stay aromatic when herbs are frozen as whole sprigs, straight off the plant.

The drawback with freezing is that the texture is rarely good on defrosting. Berries stay closest to the original, especially if frozen individually, laid on trays in single layers overnight in the freezer before decanting into bags. It helps if you keep processing to a minimum: freeze French and runner beans as they are, not even top-and-tailing them, and they stay much crisper. Spinach and its close relatives, chard and perpetual spinach, are best cooked before freezing.

Blanching is a hotly debated topic. Dropping veg into boiling water for 2-3 minutes before freezing kills enzymes that cause decay – but my frozen veg are out of the freezer and eaten long before in-freezer decay becomes an issue. So I don't blanch my veg, and I've never noticed the difference. If you're storing it for more than a few months, though, blanching will keep your veg in good condition for longer.

Dry storing

Use for: Apples; pears; root vegetables including beetroot, turnips, potatoes, carrots, celeriac.

Some produce you can just set aside till you need it, like a squirrel burying acorns for winter. Root veg are great for dry storing. Lift your whole crop, then find a slatted box, like a wine crate, and line it with breathable fabric (weed-suppressing membrane works well). Then dampen some sand just enough to stop

your roots drying out, and put a layer into the bottom of the crate. Twist off any top growth and lay your veg on the sand so they're not touching each other. Cover with more sand and they'll last like that for several months.

Potatoes are even easier: cure the skins on the soil's surface for a couple of hours in the sun after harvesting, then tip into double-thickness paper or hessian sacks to store.

Late-season apples, like 'Cox's Orange Pippin', and pears, like 'Doyenné du Comice', store best, often lasting in pretty good condition well into early spring. Save only perfect specimens and wrap them individually in

Wrap apples and pears individually to prevent rotten ones infecting their neighbours.

newspaper: rots spread quickly in storage, so check them regularly and remove any that are turning soft (if you get to them quick enough they'll still be good to eat).

MAKING PRESERVES

Master the art of making jams, chutneys and pickles, not to mention bottling (canning), and you'll turn your end-of-season veg mountain into long-lasting supplies to see you through the leanest of times.

Jam

Make perfect jam and you've arrived on the culinary scene. Jam-making is also one of the scrummiest ways of preserving large quantities of raspberries, blackberries, blackcurrants and just about any other fruit, plus some savoury produce too – home-made chilli jam turns cheese and biscuits into a total taste explosion. Jam gives you a fruity hit even in fruit-sparse months, and I'm not just talking sandwiches: it's delicious as cake and tart filling, or as hot syrup on ice cream (ideal for less-than-perfect jam that hasn't quite set).

The best fruit for jam-making is dry (never wash jam fruit) and slightly under-ripe, as the levels of pectin – the natural setting agent – are at their highest. If the fruit is in good condition, you'll only need jam sugar (with added pectin) for fruits with naturally low pectin levels, like strawberries.

Trust your instincts when making jam. You'll read stern warnings about ensuring it reaches the setting temperature of 104°C (220°F) – but whenever I've held out till then, using a jam thermometer, it's set like a brick.

A better test is the saucer trick. Put some saucers in the freezer, then when you think your jam is ready, pull one out and pop a dab of jam on it. If it wrinkles when you push it with your finger, it's ready. But best of all is watching your jam cook: when it's done, you'll know. It's an instinct you hone with experience, so make lots of jam! The beauty of home-made jam is that it doesn't have to be perfect. Syrupy, less-than-set jam tastes just as good, and even my brick-like jam found a good home in a batch or three of jam tarts.

Mastering the art of jam-making is a matter of honour for any self-respecting cook.

How to make jam

You will need:

1.5kg (3lb 5oz) fruit and an equal quantity of granulated sugar

A little butter

About 6 x 450g (1lb) screw-top jars and waxed paper (you can use the inners from cereal packets)

❋ Preheat the oven to 180°C (350°F / Gas Mark 4).

❋ Pick over the fruit and wipe off excess dirt – but don't wash it. Tip the lot into a large heavy-bottomed pan and heat gently for 10-20 minutes, until the juices start to run.

❋ While this is happening, put the sugar in a bowl and pop it in the oven to warm for 15 minutes. Once that's done, turn the heat down to 100°C (210°F / Gas Mark ¼) and sterilize your jam jars (see box on page 166).

❋ When the fruit is cooked, add the warm sugar and stir until it has dissolved

When life gives you raspberries – make jam!

Jam from frozen fruit

You can make jam from frozen fruit: the trick is not to wash it before freezing. Try mixing different kinds of fruits in the same jam just for fun.

---

completely. Now whack up the heat and boil the jam rapidly. Stir often, and start testing for a set after 10 minutes, or once you can see it's starting to thicken to a blup rather than a bubble.

❋ Take the jam off the heat to settle for 15 minutes; if there's a scum on the surface, just add a dab of butter to disperse it.

❋ Pour into the still-hot jars, cover with waxed paper discs, put the lids on and leave to cool before labelling. Home-made jam lasts several years unopened, and even once the lid's off it's good for at least 6 months if you keep it in the fridge.

Pickles

Sometimes I think the whole point of beetroot is in the pickling. I love it roasted too, but the earthy flavours are lifted to the sublime when beetroot is interlaid with raw shallots, packed into jars and pickled in hot red wine vinegar laced with black peppercorns. It takes leftover cold meats into the realms of indulgence.

Kimchi

Salting is a little-used preserving method these days, and fermenting is even less widely known. But combine the two and you've got kimchi: an explosively spicy Korean speciality. Here's an adapted version to make at home.

1 head cabbage (white, red or Chinese/ napa)
Several handfuls of sea salt
1 mooli radish
1 thumb-sized piece of ginger root
1 whole bulb of garlic
1 bunch (10-12) spring onions
Half a fresh red chilli (adjust according to taste)
2 tbsp flour

❋ Wash the cabbage, slice it lengthways and cover in salt. Put in a bowl, add a couple of cups of water and throw another handful of salt over the top. Leave overnight.

❋ Next day, rinse the cabbage thoroughly in fresh water and squeeze out any excess. Then grate the mooli and ginger and finely chop the garlic, spring onions and chilli.

❋ Mix the flour with a little water, then heat with 375ml (13fl oz) of water until it thickens. Stir in the other ingredients, then spread the resulting paste all over the cabbage.

❋ Pack into tubs to ferment at room temperature. The flavour changes gradually as it ferments – so keep tasting it, and when it's the way you like it, put it in the fridge to stall the fermenting process and enjoy.

Pickling was invented by sailors, as are most of the best things in life, and is a natural extension of salting meat on long journeys at sea. It wasn't long before someone thought the same principle could be used to keep vegetables edible (one of the great challenges of scurvy-ridden naval ships of the day) and began soaking perishable veg in vinegar to prevent them rotting. Not long after that, someone else hit on the idea of adding a few herbs and spices, and the pickle was born.

You can pickle just about anything: by all means grow pickling onions, gherkins or cornichons, and pull your beetroot very young to pickle whole, but you can also pickle sliced regular-sized vegetables as a way of preserving your surplus: particularly larger beetroot, ordinary cucumbers and summer cabbage.

Some pickles have become little short of national dishes. In the UK it's pickled onions, beetroot and the fine pub tradition of pickled eggs. In the USA, a pickle is usually a gherkin. But branch out and you can enjoy German sauerkraut (pickled cabbage) and Korean kimchi (one of the few good uses I know for winter radish, or mooli). Both add fermentation to the pickling process, just for a little extra twist.

Pickled beetroot with shallots in red vinegar – yum.

How to make pickles

You will need:

About 1kg (2lb 3oz) of your chosen vegetable: whole if they'll fit in the jar; sliced if not

Around 50-100g (2-4oz) salt if pickling onions or cabbage

1 litre (1¾ UK pints / 2 US pints) white wine vinegar for pale veg; red wine vinegar for red cabbage or beetroot

1 tsp each of your pickling spices: celery seed and mustard seed for cucumbers; coriander seed and peppercorns for onions and beetroot; bay leaves and juniper berries for red cabbage

450g (1lb) caster sugar (optional)

About 3 x 450g (1lb) Kilner or screw-top jars

❋ Some vegetables can be pickled without processing, but onions and red cabbage should be sprinkled liberally with 50-100g (about 2-4oz) salt and left to stand for 24 hours first. Rinse and dry before continuing.

❋ Put the vinegar and spices, with sugar if using, into a saucepan and slowly bring to the boil. Cook steadily for about 15 minutes, then remove from the heat and allow to cool.

❋ Pack the vegetables into sterilized, still-warm jars (see box on page 166), as tightly as possible, then pour over the vinegar mix until the vegetables are completely covered (any that are exposed to the air will go off). Cover and seal.

❋ Leave your pickles to develop their full flavour for about a month before opening. They'll keep for a year or more as long as they're sealed, but once opened, keep them in the fridge and eat within a month.

Chutney

One day I'd like to try making proper South Asian chutneys – a kaleidoscope of elaborately spiced dishes including sweet preserves and milky, yoghurty dips. But for now I'll settle for mastering just one: the brown, spicy mix of vinegar, sugar, fruit and veg that broke out of nineteenth-century colonial India to conquer European and American tastebuds.

Chutney is one of the best ways to preserve really big amounts of vegetables. It lasts for absolutely ages, and the flavours develop with time (you should always leave a newly made chutney to mellow a few months before eating it). And it's so easy that even I can make it well. You can chutney just about any-thing – from courgettes and tomatoes to rhu-barb. The only one I'm not that keen on is runner bean chutney (too lumpy).

If you're going by the book, or are just parti-cular about your flavours, make a chutney spice bag. Wrap your spices in a muslin bag, tie tightly with thread and attach to the handle of the pan so it dangles in the chutney mix. I don't always bother, adding the spices straight to the pot instead. Or there's always the really easy option: pre-mixed pickling spices are available from most grocers.

How to make chutney

You will need:
1kg (2lb 3oz) of your main vegetable
1kg (2lb 3oz) cooking apples or plums
3 large (or 4 medium) onions
500g (1lb 2oz) sultanas
500g (1lb 2oz) brown sugar
1 litre (1¾ UK pints / 2 US pints) vinegar
1 palm-sized nugget of ginger root
A quarter of a hot fresh chilli, or 1 tsp
    dried chilli flakes
1 tsp ground allspice
2 tbsp mustard seeds
1 tbsp salt
About 8 x 450g (1lb) jars

✳ Chop the vegetables and fruit into 2cm (1") dice and add to a large preserving pot or casserole dish with the sultanas, sugar and vinegar.
✳ Peel and finely chop the ginger root, then chop the chilli finely too if you're using fresh. Add these plus the allspice, mustard and salt, and give it all a really good stir (if you're using a spice bag, tie it on now).
✳ Start heating the chutney, leaving the pot uncovered. When it reaches sim-mering point, turn the heat down till it's just bubbling – not too fast, as you don't want it to burn. Leave it like this, uncovered, to cook, stirring from time to time to make sure it's not sticking.
✳ Don't believe the recipes: chutney takes far longer than the usually quoted 1½-2 hours. I've never managed it in less than 5-6 hours of steady simmering. You'll know it's ready when the fruit and veg have turned an even dark brown, the simmering becomes less of a bubble and more of a blup, and you're having to stir quite frequently so it doesn't stick.
✳ Once the mix becomes thick enough to hold a medium-weight wooden spoon upright on its own, it's ready to put into sterilized jars (see box on page 166). Leave for 3 months before eating. Chut-ney keeps in perfect condition for several years, and even once opened it's still good for several months.

Bottling (canning)

We rely so heavily on tinned food these days that it's hard to imagine life without it. Canning, also known as bottling, dates back to 1800, when it was invented by a Frenchman, Nicolas Appert, who won the 12,000-franc prize on offer to anyone who could create a way of preserving food for Bonaparte's armies.

Rediscover the art of bottling and you can forget buying all those tinned tomatoes: you can bottle your own instead. Anything that's a fruit is good for bottling, including tomatoes – but don't try to home-can non-fruiting vegetables, as you risk botulism if you get it wrong.

You'll need to get fussy about your jars for bottling, as ordinary screw-top jam jars won't form a proper seal. Use true Kilner jars – the

Capture the summer sweetness of cherries in a bottle to enjoy in the depths of winter.

ones with the two-part metal caps – or hinged jars with separate rubber seals (sterilize this kind in water, not the oven, as the rubber melts in dry heat).

Sterilizing jars

Sterilizing glass jars kills off any lurking bacteria and creates a germ-free environment to keep your preserves in perfect condition. There are three methods:

Dishwasher method: Wash jars and lids thoroughly in hot soapy water, then stack them in the dishwasher and run them on the hot cycle (without any detergent). Time the cycle so you're ready to use them just as it finishes, while they're still hot.

Oven method: Preheat the oven to about 100°C (210°F / Gas Mark ¼). Wash the jars and lids in hot water, then heat the jars in the oven for 10-15 minutes until warm and dry. Fill them while still hot, and keep the lids immersed in the hot water until needed. (You don't need to fully sterilize the lids, as they don't come in contact with the preserve thanks to the protective disc of waxed paper.)

Boiling method: After washing, put jars and lids into a large pan of cold water. Bring slowly to boiling point and simmer for 10 minutes, then remove from the heat and leave in the water until you're ready to use them.

The result is a fruit preserved more perfectly than with any other method. It keeps every nuance of flavour, and its texture too (especially if you can it whole). It's like a taste of midsummer eaten out of season: one sweetly flavoured mouthful whisks you back into endlessly lazy, sunny days of plenty, even in the chilliest, darkest depths of winter.

How to can fruit

You will need:
About 450g (1lb) fruit
115g (4oz) sugar (increase to 225g/8oz for sour fruit such as morello cherries)
600ml (about 1 UK pint / 1¼ US pints) water
2 x 0.5-litre (roughly 1-pint) Kilner jars

✳ Sterilize the jars and heat the sugar and water until it makes a syrup. Leave to cool.
✳ Keep fruit whole if possible, but if not, peel and slice. Remove any stones.
✳ Pack the fruit into the jars as tightly as you can without damaging them, then pour over the cooled syrup to fill the jar. Screw or clip on the lids, but not too tight, as glass expands on heating.
✳ Line a heavy-bottomed pan with a thick cloth, then sit the jars on top and fill the pan with cold water up to the neck of the jars. Cover with a tight-fitting lid and heat to simmering point really, really slowly – the process should take at least 1½ hours.
✳ Once it's bubbling, check the water temperature with a thermometer. The fruit must hit a certain temperature and stay there for a minimum amount of time, and it varies according to the fruit (see box below).
✳ Once you've kept them at the right temperature for the specified time, take the jars out of the water and allow to cool. Test the seal by unclipping or unscrewing the jar: if the seal stays tightly closed, it's good to keep for up to a year.

How to can tomatoes

✳ Toss 1.5kg (3lb 5oz) tomatoes in 1½ tbsp lemon juice, 1½ tsp salt and 1½ tsp sugar.
✳ Pack into jars and bring to simmering point over 1½ hours, as for other fruit (see above). Keep whole tomatoes at 88°C (190°F) for 30 minutes; halved or quartered tomatoes at that temperature for 40 minutes.

Bottling times and temperatures

Different fruits need to be kept at different temperatures and for different lengths of time for bottling, as follows:

✳ **Apples, apricots, cherries, damsons, gooseberries, peaches, plums:** 15 minutes at 82°C (180°F).
✳ **Blackberries, mulberries, raspberries:** 10 minutes at 74°C (165°F).
✳ **Pears:** 30 minutes at 88°C (190°F).

Cheers! The first sip of elderflower cordial in early summer.

Chapter Ten

GROW YOUR OWN DRINKS

" Stock your shelves with additive-free delights from just a few easy-to-grow fruits. "

What you drink is as important as what you eat. Not many people stick to water only – so if your house is anything like mine, bottles of squash lurk in the store cupboard, the fridge rattles with cartons of fruit juice and there's a bottle or three of wine lounging about waiting for the weekend. Drinks get a little forgotten in the drive for self-sufficiency – but in fact they're as easy to produce for yourself as your Sunday roast veg. Even quite sophisticated drinks like wine or cassis are only fruit plus a few extras.

It's the extras that cause the concern, of course, in commercially produced drinks. The jury is still out on bought-in squash, and some have fewer additives and sugar than others – but I know the eye-poppingly hyperactive effect they have on my kids, and all are sweeter than they need to be. With home-made versions you regain control over sugar levels and there are no additives: just pure, naturally sweet fruit.

Additives in commercial beers and wines too include a host of hidden ingredients, including sulphites, corn syrup, dextrose, acidifiers, stabilizers . . . more than I want to be knocking back on a Saturday night. Grow your own booze and you can legitimately argue that it's good for your health.

In this chapter you'll find out how to grow the five fruits which provide you with all you need for a satisfying variety of refreshing summer drinks, spritzers, tipples for the table and a pint to drink with the mates, all from your back garden. Now that's worth partying about.

CORDIAL CONCOCTIONS AND BOOZY BREWS

You can make cordials and most liqueurs using equipment you've already got in the kitchen. Each type of fruit has a relatively short season, so drop everything else and dedicate yourself to making several batches at once. Then you can decant the first into pretty glass bottles to keep in the fridge and enjoy right away, and pour the rest into large plastic drinks bottles to freeze until you need them. You can do the same with plain fruit juice too.

Making your own home-grown drinks is one of the more satisfying pastimes of self-sufficient life.

Brewing equipment can range from modern kits to glass demijohns and traditional stoneware flagons.

Home brewing is a bit more involved, so invest in some kit before you start, and brace yourself for a pretty steep learning curve. Home brews have developed a bit of a dodgy reputation over the years, sometimes justifiably – if you've ever been offered a bottle of Grandad's best home-brewed parsnip wine you'll know what I mean. But most mouth-puckeringly undrinkable home-brew mistakes are the result of impatience. Be prepared for your first efforts to end up down the sink, but keep notes and adjust quantities with each batch until you have the perfect formula. You'll need iron willpower to hold off guzzling the stuff until it's good and ready (that's years, not weeks) before you achieve the kind of boozy self-sufficiency you might actually want to have. But do keep trying: once you've opened your first really good bottle, you'll be the one with the smile on your face. And if patience isn't your strong suit, just stick to cocktails and liqueurs – so easy you're guaranteed good results first time.

Most undrinkable home brews are the result of impatience. Keep trying, until you have the perfect formula.

THE GARDEN DRINKS CABINET

You can produce a fantastic range of drinks, both alcoholic and non-alcoholic, from just five types of fruit which every gardener can grow. Some are absurdly easy: elder is a weed in my garden, and apples and blackcurrants practically look after themselves. Lemons and grapes need a little more specialist care, but your reward is home-made lemonade and proper wine.

Elder

Handsome elder trees sprout from our hedgerows like weeds and self-seed themselves in the garden. They're rather sprawling, untidy plants, but I let a few have their way, for this is the ultimate drinks plant: the sweet, pungent scent of the flowers captured in liquid

Elder can grow into a large tree in time, yielding dozens of fragrant flower sprays for cordials, wines and (best of all) 'champagne'.

form as elderflower cordial and fizzy 'champagne' takes you right back to summer the moment you uncork the bottle. Leave a few flowers on the tree, and in autumn the astringent, gleaming black berries make a rich, full-bodied wine.

Growing guide

Although it's traditional to forage elderflowers from wild trees, I prefer to grow mine in the garden. You guarantee enough flowers for your year's supply of cordial and champagne – and you're more likely to catch them at precisely the right point for processing, when the flowers have just burst their buds but aren't yet fully open.

Elder grows anywhere, in sun or shade and in any soil. They're on that fine line between large shrub and small tree, at a rangy 5-6m (16-20') tall: keep their gawky habits in bounds with a strict prune straight after flowering.

Species and varieties: Grow the species, *Sambucus nigra*, for traditional ivory-coloured cordials; the deep purple 'Black Lace' for candy-floss flowers to turn into pink 'champagne'.

Stir elderflowers, citrus, sugar and water together, steep for 24 hours, and enjoy.

25 elderflower heads
1 tbsp citric acid
1 lemon
3 limes

✳ Pour the hot water over the sugar and stir till the sugar dissolves, then leave to cool.
✳ Swish the flower heads in cold water, shake them dry, then snip the individual blooms off the stems. Tip the flowers into the sugar-and-water mix, add the citric acid and the sliced-up lemon and limes, give it all a good stir and leave covered to steep for 24 hours. Strain through muslin, then bottle.

Tip: make several batches of cordial during the short flowering season and freeze your year's supply in saved 1-litre (2-US-pint) plastic drinks bottles.

Elderflower cordial

You will need:
900g (2lb) sugar (if you prefer your cordial sweeter, you can increase this to as much as 1.8kg/4lb)
1.8 litres (about 3 UK pints / 3¾ US pints) hot water

Elderflower champagne

You will need:

25 elderflower heads

2 lemons

500g (1lb 2oz) sugar

1½ tbsp white wine vinegar

4 litres (7 UK pints / 8½ US pints) cold water

❋ Don't wash the elderflowers, but snip the individual blooms off the main stalks. Put them in a clean bucket, and add the outer rind of the lemons and their juice. Then add the sugar, vinegar and water and stir until the sugar has dissolved.

Elderflower champagne is a bit of a lottery, with explosive results if you get it wrong – but it's worth the risk.

Sterilizing bottles

Dirty bottles can ruin your brewing by interfering with fermentation in the case of brewed drinks, and introducing moulds into cordials and liqueurs. So make sure your bottles are sterilized before you put anything into them. There are a few methods you can use.

Dishwasher method: Simply put the bottles through the dishwasher on a hot cycle, and use them while they're still warm.

Oven method: Wash the bottles very thoroughly in hot water, then put them into an oven heated to 100°C (210°F / Gas Mark ¼) for about 10 minutes until they're dry.

Commercial sterilizer: Dissolve a couple of teaspoons of sterilizer (from home-brew outlets) in 4.5 litres (about 1 gallon) of warm water, and leave your bottles to soak for 10-15 minutes. Rinse well with cold water.

❋ Cover with muslin or tea towels and leave for several days until it's fizzing nicely. If it hasn't started bubbling after about 3 days, add a pinch of yeast. Bottle in thick glass flip-top bottles to minimize the risk of them exploding (which they will, spectacularly, if you use ordinary bottles). They will continue to ferment for another 2 weeks or so, so open the lid briefly every few days to take off the pressure and release excess gas.

Tip: natural yeast levels in elderflowers vary from year to year. One year you may have such fizzy elderflower champagne that your bottles are in danger of exploding, while other years you'll get more of a light spritz. Only you can tell which it is: if you're in a fizzy year, just release the gases more frequently.

Make your own cordial and you can cut back on the sugar and let the fruit flavours shine through.

Blackcurrants

There's a good reason why children find Ribena irresistible. Tart, sweet-and-sour blackcurrants explode in your mouth like little fireworks and are among my favourite fruity flavours. Yet Ribena gets a bad rap. One 500ml (1-pint) bottle of the stuff delivers 60 per cent of your daily sugar intake in one hit – the liquid equivalent of 13 chocolate biscuits.

Grow your own and you (and your kids) can have your Ribena fix without the sugary price to pay. Making your own cordial means you can cut back on the sugar without using just-as-bad artificial sweeteners, and let the fruit flavours shine through. Perhaps it's still not as healthy as a spinach smoothie, but it sure tastes better.

Tangy and sharp, blackcurrants give you your home-made Ribena fix without the sugar dilemma.

Growing guide

Blackcurrants grow whether you want them to or not. Sun or shade; rich loam or poorly drained scrubland: they don't care. These are the toughest of the tough.

Drink blackcurrant cordial with fizzy water for a special treat.

But to get the heaviest crops, spoil them. Sunshine, free-draining rich loam and winter pruning to remove old wood (blackcurrants fruit best on 2- and 3-year-old stems) keeps crops generous.

Blackcurrants must have a spell of very cold weather in the dormant season: poor crops often follow mild winters. Swollen buds which don't open mean gall mites: pick off the whole bud on sight. The only other problems are feathered . . . net plants as soon as berries turn from green to black to keep the birds off.

Varieties: Any of the 'Ben' blackcurrants will fruit copiously and reliably: 'Ben Sarek' is the choice for containers, as it's only 1m (3') tall. If you want something different, try 'Wellington XXX', said to have the best flavour of all.

Blackcurrant cordial

You will need:
800g (1lb 12oz) blackcurrants
300g (11oz) sugar (adjust quantities to
    taste)
500ml (18fl oz) water
Juice of 2 lemons

Grow your own sweetener

If you do have an irredeemably sweet tooth, try replacing some of the sugar with stevia (*Stevia rebaudiana*), an easy-to-grow but tender herb with leaves many times sweeter than sugar.

❋ De-stalk the blackcurrants, then heat them with the sugar and water in a large saucepan, stirring gently. Simmer for 5 minutes, then add the lemon juice, simmer for another 5 minutes and remove from the heat to cool.

❋ Strain through muslin and pour into glass bottles. It keeps for up to 6 weeks in the fridge (if it lasts that long!) but also freezes very well: decant into 1-litre (2-US-pint) plastic drinks bottles.

Cassis

You will need:

1.5kg (3lb 5oz) blackcurrants
2 litres (3½ UK pints / 4¼ US pints) good red wine (home-brewed if possible)
1kg (2lb 3oz) sugar (adjust to taste)
70cl (25fl oz) vodka

❋ Top and tail the blackcurrants, then mash thoroughly and stir in the wine. Cover and steep for 48 hours.

❋ Now hang up a muslin bag with a bowl underneath. You can make a simple frame on legs to hang it from, or take the seat out of a wooden chair and suspend it from that, or buy a strainer stand from a good cook shop. Pour in the mixture and leave to strain overnight.

❋ Return the resulting juice to the pan and add the sugar. Heat gently, stirring all the while, until it's just below simmering, then let it blup gently for an hour until the liquid turns syrupy.

❋ Leave to cool, then add the vodka and pour into bottles.

❋ Serve with ice cold white wine (for Kir) or champagne (for Kir Royale).

Apples

I have the extreme good fortune to live in the sublimely beautiful county of Somerset, where the word 'drink' is pronounced 'cider'. Round here grow some of the oldest and most revered cider apple varieties there are: over 150 local varieties, including several different 'Dabinett's, 'Kingston Black', 'Fair Maid of Taunton' and 'Harry Masters Jersey'. Family recipes are jealously guarded, and every Somerset household keeps a milk carton or 50 of home-made stashed in the shed.

Both cider apples and eating apples are good for juicing. A home press is one of the best ways to process a multi-kilo glut of windfalls: keep varieties separate for a connoisseur's appreciation of flavour, and freeze what you can't drink straight away.

A garden apple tree yields enough fruit to make both cider and apple juice.

Growing guide

Apples are easier to grow than you'd think, as long as you get the basics right. Always buy trees from a reputable supplier, and pay attention to the rootstock, which governs the size of the tree. Choose M9 (dwarfing) rootstock for training on a fence; MM106 for a standard apple tree. And grow at least two apple trees from the same pollination group to guarantee a good fruit set.

Prune once a year (for standard trees), aiming for a goblet shape with five main, evenly spaced branches. There are many pests and diseases which beset apples, but as long as

you water your trees in dry spells and keep them well fed and mulched with compost or well-rotted manure they should shrug off the worst.

Varieties: Though cider apples make the best cider, you can also use any of the sharper eating apples, like the dual-purpose 'James Grieve'. The best eaters and cookers for juicing include 'Howgate Wonder' (a cooker), 'Court Pendu Plat' and 'Cox's Orange Pippin'.

Apple juice

You will need:
As many apples as you can get your hands on: 2.5kg (5lb 8oz) apples makes 1 litre (1¾ UK pints / 2 US pints) of juice

❉ Wipe the apples clean, remove stalks and leaves and cut out any rotten bits (but don't remove the core or skin).

※ Chop into rough chunks and load the lot into a crusher, which will mash them into a mushy 'pomace'. Put this through a press and catch the resulting amber-brown, cloudy juice in clean buckets.

※ Pour into bottles and drink straight away (you might want to add a little water at this point, as home-made apple juice is considerably richer than the shop-bought stuff). If you make enough, you can freeze your surplus (before diluting) and keep you and your family in fresh juice year-round.

Getting your hands on crushers and presses

Both crushes and presses are widely available online, but they are a little pricey, so you might want to go into partnership with fellow apple-juicing enthusiasts.

Failing that, if you're handy with DIY it's a short weekend's work to make your own: look online and you'll find lots of different models, plus instructions on how to make them.

For another fun option, you can often get your apples juiced at a local Apple Day, held each autumn in many locations across the UK.

Cider

Real cider-making is a true art that goes back centuries: good cider makers are encyclopaedic on the subject of cider apples, able to judge the flavours produced by various variety combinations as well as any wine connoisseur. So immerse yourself in cider lore and have fun experimenting with different varieties and techniques. Here's the beginner's method.

You will need:
4.5 litres (8 UK pints / 9½ US pints) fresh apple juice (see left)
A cider home-brewing kit
Cider yeast (optional)

※ Strain the apple juice through muslin into a large, sterile bucket. Most apples will have enough yeast in the skins to kick off fermentation, but if you have trouble, a little cider yeast should do the job. Test the acidity, tannin and

Don't bother washing your windfalls: just chuck 'em in the cider vat as they come.

sweetness and adjust according to the instructions on your brewing kit.

* Pour through a funnel into a sterilized demijohn, fix an airlock and bung, and leave at room temperature (20-27°C/68-80°F) for 5-14 days: you'll know it's ready when the hydrometer reads under 1000 for a few days running. Siphon off the result into glass bottles – green or brown if you're not drinking it straight away, as light degrades the apple juice and spoils the cider.

Grapes

Grapevines are undeniably at the not-strictly-necessary end of self-sufficiency. Yes, you can do without grape juice – you can get by if you don't have a bottle of wine to uncork after work. But where's the fun in that? Growing your own is all about the luxury, and home-brewed wine is the ultimate indulgence.

Train your grapevine up a sunny wall, cover a pergola or, even better, give it a greenhouse. The venerable 240-year-old Black Hamburg vine at Hampton Court Palace in London – the world's oldest – is planted outside, the stems trained through a window for the fruits to ripen under glass. Do it this way at home and it'll fill the whole greenhouse. There won't be any room left for the tomatoes – but my, the grapes will be good.

Growing guide

Grapevines are tough and fast-growing, and quickly become very jungly: make sure you

When is cider not cider?

Don't get your cider and your apple juice confused, or you could end up with some unexpected headaches in the morning! In the UK, 'cider' refers to an alcoholic drink made by fermenting apples – sometimes known in America as 'hard cider'. In the States, 'cider' – sometimes 'sweet' or 'apple' cider – is just plain apple juice, though unfiltered, so a little cloudier.

have good supports from the start, and stay on top of training. Prune once a year in early winter before the sap rises. Grape pruning can be a highly technical affair, but in fact it's perfectly possible to train grapes to produce good harvests without knowing the intricacies of the double guyot system. Just pick one or two main stems, reduce them by a third each winter, then trim back all side shoots to a couple of buds.

The main worry is mildew, especially in hot, dry summers: it can ruin your crop. Water carefully and consistently, mulch to lock the moisture in, ventilate greenhouse grapes and don't let shoots get overcrowded.

Varieties: 'Phoenix' is reliable and mildew resistant; 'Boskoop Glory' is a good all-rounder for outdoor cultivation. But more classical wine-making choices are 'Muscat Hamburg' (red) or 'Riesling-Sylvaner' (white).

Grapes are a luxury crop – but my, they're worth growing.

Grape juice

You will need:

As many grapes as you can lay your hands
on: 450g (1lb) grapes makes 150ml
(¼ UK pint / ⅓ US pint) of juice
Sugar to taste

✳ Wash the grapes, remove the stalks
and put into a big pan. Mash them up
just enough to crush each berry, then
add water to a depth of about 5cm (2").

✳ Bring to a simmer and cook for about
10 minutes, stirring occasionally. Taste
and add sugar if you like, but most
grapes will be sweet enough without.

✳ Now strain it all through muslin and let
it cool. Grape juice doesn't freeze well,
so make small batches at a time and
drink straight away.

Wine

Don't expect the same standard as fine
grape wines – they've taken generations
of expertise to perfect. But you can have
a good crack at making something very
palatable at home. You might want to
stick to white wine in cooler climates like
the UK, as red wine grapes rarely have the
chance to ripen as fully as they need to.

You will need:

Fresh grapes: 6-7kg (about 13-15lb) grapes makes 5 litres (about 8 UK pints / 10½ US pints) wine

Good-quality wine yeast and nutrient (a basic wine-making kit)

Always follow the instructions on your wine-making kit, but the basic technique is as follows.

❋ Remove stalks, then crush the grapes. For white wine, press out the juice immediately and strain into a clean demijohn. For red wine, ferment the grapes in their skins in a clean bucket for 4-7 days first.

❋ Add wine yeast and leave at room temperature to ferment for 4-6 weeks in the demijohn, fitted with a cork and airlock. When the hydrometer reads 990-1000 for 3 days running, add one campden tablet to each gallon of red wine; two to each gallon of white wine (this helps it to keep well), then rack off into bottles and cork.

❋ Leave for as long as you can bear: white wine should be left at least 6 months, and red wine for at least a year to develop the flavours.

Getting the best from your home brew

Approach your home brewing with care, work methodically and get pernickety about the detail, and you'll avoid most of the pitfalls and will all-but-guarantee good results.

❋ **Cleanliness is next to booziness:** Don't skip the sterilizing – clean bottles, hands and brewing equipment is key to a clear, unsullied flavour, and it's all too easy to contaminate your brew.

❋ **Don't get carried away:** You can always add more, but you can't take away, so add extra ingredients like sugar, flavourings, tannin and yeast with caution.

❋ **Keep records:** Your experiments will improve year on year if you make a note of what you did when, so you can look back and see where your methods can be improved.

❋ **Be patient:** Taste your brew before you pour, and you'll know if it's ready. If you don't like it, leave it another 6 months and try again. You'll be amazed how much the flavour mellows and changes.

❋ **Make loads!** Don't wait till you start drinking one batch before you make the next, or you'll have a dry year or two to wait. Make a brew every month or two to keep the supply coming.

Vegetable wine

No, don't laugh: I know exactly what you're thinking. But honestly, wine made with vegetables is absolutely delicious when it's done well – and it's a fantastic way to use up surplus produce.

The best wine-making vegetable is parsnip – the result is sweet yet smoky, and richly smooth as long as you leave it at least 2 years (and preferably 5 or more) to age properly. But you can also use beetroot, rhubarb, marrows and carrots.

2.25kg (5lb) vegetables
4.5 litres (8 UK pints / 9½ US pints) water
1.3kg (3lb) sugar
Juice of 1 orange
Juice and zest of 2 lemons
Good-quality wine yeast and nutrient (a basic wine-making kit)

* Scrub the veg, then top-and-tail them and chop roughly into chunks without peeling. Put them into a pan, add the water and bring to the boil. Simmer for about 15-20 minutes, until soft but not mushy.
* Strain through muslin into a clean bucket, then stir in the sugar until dissolved.
* Cool overnight, then add yeast and the other ingredients and leave to ferment for 4 days, stirring every day. Strain into a sterilized demijohn, top up with cold water if necessary, and fix an airlock and bung.
* Once it's bubbled away for a few weeks, siphon into a fresh demijohn and then leave for about 6 months to finish fermenting before you bottle it.

Lemons (and other citrus)

Crack the demands of growing citrus, which can be temperamental when too cold (i.e. most of the time in the UK), and they're remarkably productive. Self-sufficiency in, say, orange juice is perhaps a tall order unless you're up for moving to Florida. But even in cooler climates it's perfectly possible to grow the handful of fruit required for lemon zest to make the scrummy Italian cocktail limoncello. And if you grow two or three trees you'll get a respectable crop, enough for all the home-made lemonade you need; zingy and refreshingly different from over-sweetened fizzy shop-bought stuff. Or you could make lemon or lime cordial for a vitamin-packed kids' favourite.

Growing guide

Lemons are among the easiest citrus to grow in cooler climates, especially grafted on to cold-tolerant trifoliate orange (*Poncirus trifoliata*) rootstocks. Grow them in containers, as you'll need to move them into a frost-free greenhouse or conservatory through winter (do this gradually, or they'll lose their leaves). Citrus survive temperatures down to -5°C (23°F), but not happily: they're healthier kept at 5°C (41°F) or above year-round.

Move them (gradually) outdoors for summer into the warmest, sunniest spot you have, as citrus trees under cover are plagued by pests, from scale insects to red spider mite: keep humidity high and wipe the leaves regularly to discourage infestations. Water sparingly, and don't stint on the feed during summer.

Species and varieties: Lemon 'Four Seasons' crops reliably, carrying sweetly scented blossom and bright yellow fruits on the plant at the same time. The juiciest lime is the Tahiti lime (*Citrus* x *latifolia*) – though turn up the thermostat to keep it happy.

Lemonade

You will need:
6 large lemons
150g (5oz) sugar
1.4 litres (2½ UK pints / 3 US pints) boiling water

❋ Use a potato peeler to thinly remove the yellow zest from the lemons. Make sure you don't bring any white pith with it, or it will turn the lemonade bitter.

❋ Juice the lemons, then put zest, lemon juice and sugar into a large bowl. Pour over the boiling water, stir and cover, before leaving overnight to steep. Next day, strain the lemonade through muslin and bottle it. It's best drunk chilled and fresh, but it'll keep happily in the fridge for up to 10 days. You can also freeze any surplus.

Tip: if you prefer your lemonade fizzy, dilute with sparkling water or soda water.

Limoncello

You will need:
5 lemons
1 litre (1¾ UK pints / 2 US pints) vodka
200g (7oz) white sugar
425ml (¾ UK pint / ⁹/₁₀ US pint) water

❋ Soak your lemons overnight in cold water to soften the skins, then remove the zest with a potato peeler. Put this into a large jar and pour over the vodka. Seal and shake, then leave to infuse for a month, giving it an occasional stir.

❋ Dissolve the sugar in the water, bring to the boil for a minute or so, then leave to cool. Mix this syrup with your vodka-and-lemon infusion, shake well and strain through muslin into clean bottles.

Lemons steeping in vodka for my favourite home-grown liqueur.

A few lavender bushes is all you need for a home-grown stress buster.

Chapter Eleven

THE BACKYARD MEDICINE CABINET

> "Boost your health, treat everyday ailments and pamper yourself - with the secret cornucopia in your own back garden."

One of my favourite shops in the world, right up there with any John Lewis department store and the Paul Bocuse bread shop in Lyon, France, is the herbalist's shop tucked away in a little square in Glastonbury, in the south-west of England. You go back in time about 500 years the moment you walk through the door. The walls are lined with shelves of potion bottles and hundreds of mysterious wooden drawers, each carefully labelled by hand, full of strange powders and fragments of plant. When you pull them open they release little puffs of fragrance – some headily sweet, some spicy, some bitterly pungent. It's the sort of place where you wouldn't be surprised to find Professor Sprout from Hogwarts behind the till.

Pretty feverfew is an effective cure for headaches.

grow your own medicine cabinet and beauty parlour, adding yet another string to your self-sufficiency bow.

HERBAL LORE

Herbs are magic plants. The secret substances they store in leaves, stems and roots are so powerful that they can clear digestive problems or send us to sleep with no more than a stem steeped in boiling water.

The search for exactly what it is in these little plants that makes them so powerful, and how to harness that power, is still going on today, but the truth is that such substances form the basis of much modern medicine. Whatever your views on herbal and homeopathic treatments, the boundaries between these and conventional medicine are more blurred than your doctor may like you to think. Historic houses donate their yew clippings for taxol,

In that charming shop there's a mind-boggling range of plants, with a kaleidoscope of uses. You can buy dried lavender for relaxation and wormwood for repelling insects; willow bark extract to treat arthritis and tincture of feverfew to combat migraines. You can lure in a lover with a sprig of fennel and repel an enemy with a flick of eucalyptus oil. There are plants here I'd never heard of, and others with familiar names used in very unfamiliar ways. And nine out of ten of them would be perfectly at home in your back garden.

This chapter is all about harnessing the power of plants to heal the body and to help you feel good. Here you'll discover how to

We barely understand what it is about plants that makes them so powerful.

a chemotherapy drug used to fight cancer; and daffodils are grown by the field-full in the Black Mountains in Wales, where they're developing a treatment for Alzheimer's using galantamine – a chemical found in abundance in daffodil bulbs.

Cosmetics, too, may have moved a long way from their roots, but the first hair dyes, eye shadows and skin softeners were all derived from plants. Home-made cosmetics are often more subtle than commercial products, with more gentle, natural-looking results – and they're also kinder to your skin and hair.

HERBS FOR HEALTH

The art of growing medicines is among the oldest branches of gardening. The first herbal was written nearly 5,000 years ago, in China, and Egyptian papyri dating back to 2800 BC record the medicinal uses of marjoram, mint

Blend different herbs for remedies to a range of ailments, from coughs to indigestion.

and juniper. Monastery 'physic' gardens grew mainly medicinal herbs – living pharmacies where you could get cures for all sorts of ailments. And in medieval gardens, from the humblest peasant's cottage to the grandest castle, recipes for cures, fumigants and tonics were handed down from generation to generation – at a time when it was taken for granted that if you needed medicine, you reached into the garden.

When printing came along, the study of medicinal herbs blossomed, as the monks' manuscripts, previously copied painstakingly by hand, could be reproduced more widely. Herbals like Gerard's *Herball*, published in 1597, and Culpeper's *Complete Herbal*, published in 1653, collected together the wisdom of ages. They're still bibles for medicinal herbalists today.

Much of that wealth of knowledge, though, is lost to us now. The commercialization of medicine means we are more likely to pick up a cough medicine in a pharmacy than reach for a sprig of sage to infuse in boiling water for a gargle. We take aspirin for headaches, unaware that the feverfew plant flowering away in a forgotten corner of the garden has as much (some would argue more) power to heal. But now, with a little help from those dusty old herbals and a renewed interest in natural healing, we're starting to rediscover how to use plain old plants to treat ailments from coughs to indigestion and migraines to eczema.

You may want to give some of the more eccentric treatments out there a miss – I'm not sure I'll ever get the urge (or the time) to

Grow your own tea garden

Tisanes or infusions, also known as herbal teas, are one of the most common ways to take medicinal herbs. They take no longer to make than a cup of ordinary tea. Drink three to four cups a day for the full effect.

Plant the herbs you use most often in herbal teas in a tea garden in a sunny spot near the back door, where you can just reach out and grab a sprig to make your cuppa. Here are ten herbs you could include: mix and match for a pretty and productive little garden.

Chamomile: Not to absolutely everyone's taste, but invaluable for a calming before-bed drink. Use German chamomile (*Matricaria recutita*) or Roman or common chamomile (*Chamaemelum nobile*).

Echinacea: These lovely dusky-pink flowers make a great all-purpose health booster,

source all 70-plus herbal ingredients for Venice treacle, a seventeenth-century remedy for headaches, let alone the 5 pints of sack you need to infuse it with. Especially since nobody's sure it worked all that well. But there's every reason to keep an aloe vera plant on the windowsill, so you can snap off a piece in a trice to soothe a burnt finger; or rustle up some comfrey ointment ready for rubbing into aching backs or soothing bumps and bruises.

However: a word of warning. Herbal remedies are not invariably better, or even always as good as, conventional medicine. So, perhaps more than in any other area of self-sufficiency, be self-reliant as far as is sensible but know where to draw the line. What's more, herbs can, used unwisely, do you harm: plants are more powerful than you imagine, and the medicines derived from them are often very potent. So stick to the simple stuff, and go to your doctor as usual for the rest.

A cup of herbal tea: the chance to put your feet up, with benefits.

chopped and added to boiled water (two teaspoonfuls of fresh flower, or one of dried). An easy-to-grow perennial.

Lemon balm (*Melissa officinalis*): A lovely refreshing lemony tea to help with insomnia, anxiety and indigestion – the perfect nightcap to soothe you to sleep. It's also delicious cold with ice and a twist of mint leaf. And it's super-easy to grow: unlike lemon verbena, it's hardy.

Lemon verbena (*Aloysia triphylla*): Has a delicious lemony tang which makes for a refreshing tea, with slightly sedative, soothing side-effects. The herb is frost-tender, so bring it indoors for winter.

Pot marigold (*Calendula officinalis*): Vibrant orange marigold flowers are powerful healers: in a tea, they help relieve digestive troubles such as irritable bowel syndrome and colitis. An easy-going hardy annual.

Rosemary: Some swear by a cup of rosemary tea each morning to stave off memory loss: it's also a good stimulating pick-me-up to get you going in the morning. A hardy, easy and evergreen herb.

Sage: Soothing for coughs and sore throats – you can use the infusion as a gargle too. An easy-to-grow evergreen herb: give it a haircut in late spring to keep it neat, and replace your plants every 3-4 years with new ones from softwood cuttings, as they get leggy with age.

Spearmint (*Mentha spicata*): Probably the most popular herbal tea of all, best drunk after a good meal, when it aids digestion. Grow in a container sunk in the ground to prevent it spreading too invasively.

Lemon balm is a bit of a cure-all – antiseptic, antiviral and antibiotic. And it grows like a weed.

St John's wort (*Hypericum perforatum*): Dry the flower to keep through winter, as it's a mild anti-depressant and great for those who suffer the winter blues. A straightforward hardy shrub.

Herbs for preventing disease

You probably already have some of these plants growing in your garden, unless you've been super-efficient and weeded out all your nettles lately. A regular dose of these preventative herbs keeps most niggly illnesses at bay. Some are delicious too: with a bottle of rosehip syrup in the fridge, taking your medicine becomes a positive pleasure.

✳ **Echinacea:** Infuse two teaspoons of fresh petals in boiling water for an immune-system-boosting drink.
✳ **Nettles (*Urtica dioica*):** Pick the young tops and make into a tisane that's a bracing

tonic of vitamin C and iron.

* **Rosemary:** Energizing and revitalizing: a few sprigs in the bath peps you up before a good night out.
* **Roses:** Use the hips (*Rosa glauca* has the fattest ones) to make rosehip syrup, packed with vitamin C.
* **Thyme:** Antibacterial, antiviral and a fantastic treatment for coughs, colds and chest infections: steep in boiling water to make a tea (but brace yourself for a less-than-pleasant flavour). It's evergreen, so will keep you supplied in winter.

Roses for remedies

The apothecary's rose, *Rosa gallica* var. *officinalis*, has been used as a herb for centuries (hence the name) and is still the best choice for perfumes, cosmetics and medicinal uses.

Ways with medicinal herbs

Extracting the good stuff from your medicinal herbs usually involves a little processing. The simplest procedures involve no more than boiling water, but you can get as sophisticated as you like as you get more into making your own medicines. The more complicated preparations are less self-sufficient, as you're using materials like glycerine, vodka and emulsifiers – but as always, it's up to you how purist you want to be.

Infusions (tisanes): Put a generous sprig 8-10cm (3-4") long, or two teaspoonfuls of fresh herbs (or one teaspoonful of dried) in a teapot or cup and cover with boiling water. Steep for 10-15 minutes, strain and drink.

Decoctions: For roots, bark and seeds.

Wash and chop, then add one teaspoonful of chopped herb to one cup of water. Bring to the boil and simmer for 10-15 minutes. Strain, allow to cool, then drink.

Tinctures: Place 300g (10½oz) of fresh herbs (or 100g/3½oz of dried) in a jar, add 250ml (8¾fl oz) of vodka, and leave to steep for a month on a sunny windowsill, shaking gently each day.

Ointments: Melt 150g (5¼oz) of emulsifying wax in a glass bowl set in a pan of boiling water. Add 70g (2½oz) of glycerine, 80ml (2¾fl oz) of water and 75g (2¾oz) of fresh herbs (or 30g/1oz dried). Stir and simmer for 3 hours, strain through a jelly bag, and stir slowly and continuously until it cools and sets.

Rosehip syrup

You will need:

900g (2lb) rosehips, picked just as they start to soften

450g (1lb) sugar

2.5 litres (4½ UK pints / 5½ US pints) water

Glass bottles with lids

❊ Bring 3 UK pints (3½ US pints) of water to the boil, and chop up the rosehips as fine as you can with a food processor (there's no need to top-and-tail them). Add the minced rosehips to the boiling water and turn up the heat until it's on a good fast boil, then remove from the heat and leave to stand for 15 minutes.

❊ Pour into a jelly bag or muslin square and allow the liquid to drip through.

❊ Boil the remaining water and add the pulp left over from the straining process. Again bring to a fast boil, remove from the heat and let it sit for 15 minutes, then strain it through the muslin.

❊ Heat the oven to 75°C (165°F) and put the glass bottles in it for 10 minutes to sterilize them. Wash the lids in very hot water too.

❊ Now take all the strained liquid and bring it to the boil. Add the sugar and boil rapidly for another 5 minutes. Then pour into the glass bottles (they should still be hot) and seal immediately. Keep your bottles somewhere cool and dark and they're good for up to 4 months – though once you've opened it, keep your syrup in the fridge and consume within a week.

Packed with vitamin C, rosehip syrup is a great excuse for including flowers in the veg garden.

Herbs for treating coughs and colds

Why is it that colds strike on a Friday, just in time to ruin your weekend fun? Or just on the day you've got some crucial presentation to give at work and need to be at your best? It takes minutes to stew up a few home-grown remedies – here are five of the best – to chase away the worst symptoms. Even better, concoct a warm, comforting, cold-busting drink to perk you up and help you feel ready for anything.

❊ **Borage (*Borago officinalis*):** An infusion of the leaves, as a tisane or sponge wash, cools down fevers.

❊ **Chilli peppers:** Warming and stimulating to get the circulation going and clear the sinuses.

Borage is a cooling herb, good when you've got a fever.

* **Eucalyptus:** Dry the leaves and simmer in water, then breathe in the fumes to clear your head.
* **Peppermint (*Mentha* x *piperita*):** The essential oils include menthol and act as expectorants and decongestants: infuse in hot water and breathe in the steam to clear blocked noses and soothe sore throats.
* **Yarrow (*Achillea millefolium*):** Infuse in water for 5 minutes for a tisane to gently sweat out a fever.

A cold-busting herbal drink

You will need:
1 tsp dried peppermint leaves
1 tsp dried yarrow
1 tsp dried elderflowers
1 tsp lemon juice
570ml (1 UK pint / 1¼ US pints) boiling water
Honey to taste (optional)

Mix the herbs and lemon juice in a bowl and pour over the boiling water. Infuse for at least 5 minutes, then filter through a tea strainer. Add a little honey to sweeten if you like, and enjoy. This mix soothes and warms, and at the same time induces a gentle sweat, helping to reduce a fever.

Herbs for treating injuries

The art of poulticing is largely forgotten these days, unless you own a horse. It's a bit messy, but very effective (see box on next page). Herbs with antibacterial properties prevent infection too: keep a bottle of simple antiseptic wound wash in the fridge, and next time the kids come in with bloodied knees, you'll be primed and ready to mop up.

* **Aloe vera:** An incredibly useful succulent for the kitchen windowsill – the gummy sap from a cut leaf heals burns and is an effective treatment for infected wounds.
* **Comfrey:** Its traditional name is 'knitbone'.

Comfrey is also known as 'knitbone', for its ability to heal sprains and bruises.

Pulverize the leaves for a poultice to soothe sprains and bruises.

❋ **Lavender:** Antiseptic and soothing, lavender helps heal burns, stings and cuts.

❋ **Parsley:** Use leaves or roots as a poultice for sprains, wounds and insect bites.

❋ **St John's wort (*Hypericum perforatum*):** A poultice of flowers and leaves eases burns, bruises and pain.

Antiseptic wound wash

You will need:
A large double handful of fresh elder leaves
1 litre (1¾ UK pints / 2 US pints) water
2-3 bottles or jars

Cover the leaves in the water and bring to a gentle simmer, then cook gently for 15 minutes, with the lid on the pan. Leave to cool without taking the lid off, then strain and bottle the infusion in sterilized glass bottles or jars. It'll keep for several weeks in the fridge. Use to clean and disinfect grazes and cuts prior to dressing them.

How to make a poultice

Poultices are an old traditional method of drawing out infection, pain and swelling from wounds, burns and bruises. They're easy to make and really effective for quick and effective first aid. You just need half a cup of herb – such as comfrey, St John's wort (*Hypericum perforatum*), arnica (*Arnica montana*) or yarrow (*Achillea millefolium*) – and 1 cup of water.

Simmer the herb in the water for a couple of minutes, then mush the whole lot up in a food processor or by hand using a mortar and pestle. Drain off excess liquid to leave a thick paste.

Once you have your herbal mix, either spread it, still warm, direct on to the area (the messy option) or apply a layer of gauze, then spread the poultice mixture, then cover with a second layer of gauze and bandage in place. Another method is to fill a muslin bag with the mixture, then secure that over the wound.

Change the poultice about four times a day – and if the wound doesn't start healing or develops an infection, see a doctor.

HERBS FOR BEAUTY

Ever tried putting cucumber slices on tired eyes to bring back a little sparkle? There – you're using home-made cosmetics already. Making your own beauty treatments from plants you've grown in the garden is where self-sufficiency crosses the line into naked self-indulgence. Fill your bath with the calming scents of lavender, steep your feet in a reviving bath of rosemary, cleanse your skin with sweetly scented chamomile flowers and you'll feel like Cleopatra.

Of course, home-grown cosmetics are limited in comparison to the high-tech wizardry on offer from cosmetic companies. But perhaps we've become a little too wedded to potions and lotions full of artificial chemicals and perfumes, many of which are shorter-lasting and harsher on hair and skin than home treatments. You don't have to give up your favourite anti-wrinkle cream and watch the crows' feet deepen, though. As always, it's all about becoming self-sufficient where you can.

I prefer to be purist about my home-grown cosmetics, so I've stuck to ingredients you

Many commercial potions and lotions are harsher on the skin and hair than home treatments.

* **Catmint (*Nepeta* x *faassenii*):** The leaves soothe the scalp and encourage hair growth.
* **Rhubarb:** The roots, dried or pulped, make a blonde hair dye.
* **Sage:** Add to herbal shampoo infusions to condition and darken hair colour.
* **Soapwort (*Saponaria officinalis*):** Use both leaves and roots to cleanse and freshen.
* **Southernwood (*Artemisia abrotanum*):** The infused leaves encourage hair growth and help prevent dandruff.

can find in the garden. Bought-in oils and waxes expand the range of cosmetics you can make, and it's a lot of fun to play with home-made soaps, marigold-petal face cream and wax-based lip balms. But it's hardly self-sufficient if it involves a trip to the chemist's to buy a small suitcase full of lanolin, glycerine and borax to make them. So I stick to home-grown for a bathroom cupboard stocked, by and large, from what I can grow.

Herbs for shampoos and hair treatments

There's nothing like using garden plants to wash your hair for making you feel like you've landed the lead in a Timotei advert. A good basic shampoo made from easy-to-grow soapwort doesn't froth up like bought shampoos, but then suds are mainly there for theatre – your hair still comes out clean. Add medicinal herbs for scalp problems, and dyeing herbs to darken or lighten your colour naturally.

Soapwort shampoo

You will need:

1 tbsp chopped soapwort leaves and stems, or grated root

A handful of fresh herbs: chamomile flowers for light-coloured hair; sage for darker hair; southernwood for treating dandruff; stinging nettles as conditioner

285ml (½ UK pint / ⅔ US pint) boiling water

Put the soapwort and herbs into a bowl and pour over the boiling water. Leave it to infuse until cool, then strain and use. This produces enough for about three hair washes.

Herbs for bath oils and scents

We all love a long, luxurious soak in the bath. But with jars of dried scented and therapeutic herbs in the bathroom, you'll raise your occasional treat to all-out luxury indulgence. Relax just before bed in a mist of lavender, or wake yourself up when you're feeling a bit

Fill the air with the soft scent of lavender for a soothing, relaxing, end-of-the-day bath.

* **Meadowsweet (*Filipendula ulmaria*):** This damp meadow wildflower has a soothing, slightly sedative effect.
* **Rosemary:** An invigorating and mildly disinfecting herb for wake-me-up morning baths.
* **Scented-leaved pelargoniums:** Geraniums with powerfully perfumed leaves smelling of peppy citrus, apples and mint, or soothing, restful roses.

An invigorating bath bag

You will need:

3 tbsp pot marigold (*Calendula officinalis*) petals
3 tbsp mint leaves
2 tbsp grated lovage root
1 tbsp pine needles

Mix the herbs together in a basin, then tip into a piece of muslin. Tie at the top, then tuck into the toe of a nylon stocking. Hang under the hot water tap while you're running the bath to release the herbs' powerful scents and aromatic oils. If you dry it out in an airing cupboard afterwards, you can reuse it several times.

morning-after-the-night-beforeish with a zingy mix of invigorating herbs and you'll be bouncing out of your bath ready for your day.

* **Lavender:** Releases a relaxing, soothing scent perfect for bathing.
* **Lovage:** The grated root added to a bath bag along with other herbs has a deodorant effect.

Herbs for skin tonics

Skincare is top of the list when it comes to cosmetics. But when you have sensitive skin like I do, off-the-shelf treatments are a lottery, and too often my face has been left smarting. But with home-made cosmetics I can adjust the strength till I've got a tailor-made product for me. Do a 'test patch' first, to see how your skin reacts, then remix as needed.

Use witch hazel with care – it can be quite astringent.

Steam your skin clean

For a refreshing skin tonic, stir a handful of fresh chamomile flowers into a bowl of boiling water. Hold your face over the top under a towel for 10 minutes to cleanse, soften and tone your skin.

* **Chamomile (*Chamaemelum nobile* or *Matricaria recutita*):** The flowers are gently cleansing and a little astringent.
* **Elder:** The flowers are softening, soothing and cleansing.
* **Lady's mantle (*Alchemilla mollis*):** The leaves are healing, astringent and reduce inflammation.
* **Roses:** The petals are beautifully scented, cleansing and gently astringent.
* **Witch hazel (Virginian is best – *Hamamelis virginiana*):** The distilled bark cleanses, soothes and heals.

Cleansing rosewater and witch hazel facial tonic

You will need:
450g (1lb) witch hazel bark
2 cups tightly packed with rose petals

* Start by making the witch hazel extract. Put the bark in a pot and cover with water. Bring to the boil, turn down the heat and simmer for 20 minutes. Allow to cool, then strain through muslin (if you stop here, witch hazel tonic makes a great skin toner, but it is quite astringent so use for oily skins only).
* Next, make your rosewater by putting the petals in a pan and covering with about 2¼ cups of water. Simmer gently, uncovered, until the water has reduced by about half. Then allow to cool and strain through muslin.
* A mix of about five parts rosewater to three parts witch hazel makes a good general-purpose skin tonic and cleanser, but the beauty of home-made cosmetics is that you can adjust as necessary. If you find it's too sharp for your skin, add more rosewater; if you need a more cleansing action, bump up the witch hazel.

Home-grown beanpoles have knobbly bits in all the right places for climbing beans and peas.

Chapter Twelve
THE HOME-GROWN GARDEN SHED

"Save yourself a car journey by growing your own gardening materials. They'll look much more stylish too."

Much as I love a good retail therapy session down at the garden centre, there's an awful lot of stuff involved with this gardening malarkey. You need only be at it a few weeks before you're drowning in plastic pots and your shed is bulging with an A-Z of horticultural gizmos, much of which you didn't really need: apple pickers, bulb planters, canes, dibbers, edging irons, fertilizers, gloves, hats, irrigation kits, jute twine, kneelers . . . you get the picture.

I reuse and recycle where I can: some particularly resilient plastic pots have raised years of seedlings for me, and all our cardboard loo-roll inners end up filled with compost and turned into ersatz broad bean seed modules. Any sizeable sheet of clear polythene is press-ganged into cloche covers, newspapers roll into sturdy little degradable pots, and plastic margarine tubs make great plant labels. But nobody wants a garden that looks like a junk yard, and sometimes you just need new,

Home-grown design

Some things are just far more beautiful grown and made at home anyway. There's a unique, artless charm to the home-made that sits far better in a natural-looking garden than does a modern off-the-shelf design. This originality is the kind of stuff you see on the style pages of glossy magazines, and you can't buy it in the shops without taking out a second mortgage. Yet if you grow your own, you can have it for free. Here are a few design ideas with an artistic twist, using the home-grown materials described in this chapter.

* Brighten up your hazel wigwams by weaving willow whips in contrasting colours among the uprights. Young willow comes in lots of colours: make broad, evenly spaced stripes of the same or alternating colours, or mix them up into a rainbow.
* Use coloured varieties of New Zealand flax to make purple, red or bright green string, and use them to lash together bamboo canes driven into the ground as a criss-cross fence. The contrast of bright colours and pale bamboo is a real eye-catcher.
* Make a sweet-pea arch out of 1-year-old hazel whips, tied together at the top. Choose four whips, no more than 1cm (½") diameter and about 1.8m (6')

tall. Poke them into the ground at the corners of a square, then twist the tops together in pairs so they cross over and make a simple arch.

* Split bamboo canes to make stylish, rot-resistant plant labels which you can just sand off at the end of the season and reuse. Cut a hollow cane into short 15-20cm (6-8") lengths, then split lengthways into three pieces. Sand the edges smooth, carve the end into a gentle point and it's ready to write.

Twiggy hazel whips woven into arches look so natural they blend into the background – letting the flowers take centre stage.

whether it's string, plant supports, fertilizer or a pretty edging to a veg bed. These days, though, instead of setting off for the garden centre I'm more likely to reach out and pick my own.

In this chapter I'll suggest the best plants you can grow to provide yourself with a lifetime's supply of plant supports, string, fertilizer, potting compost and plant labels – in short, all your day-to-day veg-growing needs. Once you're growing your own garden sundries, with everything you need within reach, it's my guess your trips to the garden centre will become less and less frequent. Not only is that better for the environment: you'll have a much tidier shed.

Grow hazel in your garden, and it's a satisfying winter job to cut your beanpoles for the coming year.

FIVE OF THE BEST GARDEN-SHED PLANTS

These five plants are all you need to grow to keep your garden shed supplied year-round with gardening materials and plant feed. Though you can't eat them, they'll more than earn their place in the garden. And besides, most will thrive in those awkward shady, damp or stony corners where nothing else will grow, so you don't need to give up good veg-growing space to include them. What's not to like?

Hazel

Good for: Woven edging, hurdle fencing, beanpoles, pea sticks, wigwams, arches.

Hazel is my go-to garden sundries plant. I love having it in the garden for its yellow spring

Voilà! Hazel poles make perfect supports for climbing beans to scramble up.

catkins and handsome leaves, and it's alive with wildlife scampering about and stealing nuts. But it's so extraordinarily useful that I have to sit on my hands each year or I'd strip out every single branch. It supports my beans, props up my peas, sends sweet peas and squash scrambling over my head and gives drunken late-season sprouts and globe artichokes something to lean on.

Coppicing hazel is an ancient forestry practice, originally used for charcoal-burning and livestock fencing, and exploits hazel's natural tendency to send up a thicket of arrow-straight stems from a central base, or bole. The 1-year-old hazel stems are whippy and ideal for weaving; within 3 years they're slender 2-3cm (1")-diameter canes, great for wigwams. By 5 years old, the poles are a good 5cm (2") across and able to hold up arches and the heaviest of beans and frame-woven hurdle fencing.

Hazel is great for filling a difficult spot in the veg garden or allotment. If you've room, grow three, five or more trees to crop in rotation. Harvest one tree a year, and they'll give you a succession of stems of different ages and thicknesses. Or, if you don't like the shorn effect of a fully coppiced tree, harvest a few stems from each tree every year, leaving the rest to grow on, so you get different thicknesses on the same bole.

Growing and using

Hazel is such an easy-going plant that it'll grow anywhere: sun or shade, damp or dry. But for the fastest growth, give it good, free-draining soil and at least partial sunshine.

Use the twiggy ends of hazel to support peas too.

Left to their own devices, hazel trees grow quite large, but coppiced hazel stays neat and rarely reaches more than about 3m (10') tall. To coppice a hazel, wait 2-3 years while the tree establishes, then, once it's growing strongly, cut stems cleanly down to the ground in late winter or early spring. The tree responds with a flush of new, straight stems.

How to make an A-frame bean support

You will need:
Several pairs of hazel poles, coppiced from a 3- or preferably 5-year-old plant, around 5cm (2") in diameter
String
Climbing bean plants

Put up supports just after sowing your climbing beans, so they're in place well before they're needed.

✳ Cut your beanpoles to roughly equal lengths: about 2.4m (8') supports French and runner beans as well as the taller varieties of pea.

✳ Drive them firmly into the ground in pairs, 45-60cm (1'6"-2') apart and angled towards each other, so they cross over at the top. Then cut a single pole to rest across them all in the 'X' formed by the crossing pairs.

✳ Bind uprights and cross-pole together firmly with string. Each upright supports two or three bean plants. Poles can be reused, but become increasingly brittle with age: replace with fresh as required.

Willow

Good for: Obelisks, edging, fencing, sculpture, dens, Christmas wreaths, tunnels, arches.

Second only to hazel for construction projects, the elegant, slender-leaved willow grows like a weed in damp soil. On the Somerset Levels it has fuelled an entire industry, harvested for centuries to make baskets and fences, while more recent uses include artist's charcoal and willow sculptures.

Willow roots enthusiastically the moment it touches the ground, and deeply too. Stick cut willow into the ground for your beans to climb up, and next time you look you'll have an impromptu willow thicket where your beans used to be. That's not always bad: living willow fences are beautiful and strong too, the criss-crossed stems naturally grafting to each other at the joins. But all that exuberance needs constant supervision – you'll be trimming your fence as often as a hedge. So I keep my willow strictly above ground, where it is far more well-behaved and looks very fetching woven among (non-rooting) hazel uprights.

Best of all, willow construction comes in technicolour. The two standard weaving willows are *Salix viminalis*, with super-long, strong shoots in a pleasing lime-yellow, and *S. triandra* 'Black Maul', in rich maroon-brown. But in the garden you can add the waxy *S. x fragilis* 'Flanders Red', which dries to a dusky orange, or the ebony-black *S. nigricans*. Then there's greeny-yellow *S. alba* var. *vitellina* and the lovely *S. alba* var. *vitellina* 'Britzensis', in

Living willow is lovely and strong – but close refereeing is needed to keep it within bounds.

brick-red. Grow two or three varieties and have a ball weaving yourself stripy wigwams, fences and bed edgings.

Growing and using

Willow does best in damp soil, so choose your lowest, wettest spot and stand well back. If your garden is on the dry side, try digging a deep hole and lining it with old compost sacks or a pond liner to hold water, then backfill it with soil and plant into that.

Otherwise willow is an unfussy plant: coppice it just like hazel in winter or early spring; on a 1-year cycle for weaving, or a 3-year cycle for sturdier stems to use for uprights and cross-bars in fencing.

How to make a woven willow tunnel

You will need:
Hazel poles about 1.2m (4') tall
Plenty of whippy willow stems, as long as possible
String

✳ Sink the hazel poles firmly into the ground along each side of the tunnel, spacing them about 60cm (2') apart. Then tie two or three willow stems to the top of each hazel upright in a bundle, winding string around the length so they're tightly bound in.
✳ Next, weave together each bundle of willow with the one opposite it, crossing them over your head to make a series of arches. Then use more willow

Keeping your willow flexible

If you can't use your willow straight away, prevent the newly cut stems drying out by floating them in the pond – keeping them damp and flexible until you need them.

to weave in and out of the uprights, making evenly spaced bands about 15cm (6") wide, locking the uprights together into a sturdy structure.

Willow tunnels are a lovely way of showing off climbing beans and sweet peas, but my favourite use for them is to support climbing squash like 'Tromboncino', so the fruits can dangle fetchingly off the tunnel as they grow.

Willow woven through hazel works beautifully.

Bamboo

Good for: Beanpoles, wigwams, fencing, trellis, screens, plant labels, bamboo shoots, dibbers, wildlife homes, wind chimes.

Bamboo is a designer's favourite: tall, elegant, and pleasingly swishy in a light breeze. And it's so incredibly useful in the garden: strong and attractive enough for really smart, straight fencing. It splits satisfyingly along its length: use short half-round lengths as dibbers to transplant seedlings, or split further into flat blades of strong wood you can use as plant labels. It's even edible, if you can be bothered to peel the tough bamboo shoots that appear in ever-wider circles each spring.

And there's the problem. I have never yet come across a bamboo which hasn't developed a

dedication to invasion that Genghis Khan himself would have envied. I have seen bamboos push over walls, punch holes in ponds, tunnel under fences and lift paving. If you must plant bamboo, make sure you stick to marginally less troublesome species like *Fargesia*, *Chusquea* or *Thamnocalamus*.

But if you can cope with the niggling feeling that you're under siege, bamboo quickly becomes indispensible as a crop to harvest for gardening. You'll soon find yourself cutting a culm most times you're outside – for propping up peas, lacing into trellis for the kiwi vine or, cut into 15cm (6") lengths, as a handy dibber for making holes to plant your leeks or strike herb cuttings. Just don't take your eyes off it for long, that's all.

Growing and using

Plant bamboo anywhere in the garden, but keep it in bounds. Root restrainers – 45cm (18") vertical barriers or bags of thick fabric, often coated in copper and latex to stop roots getting through – will hold a plant back for a few years if you sink them deep into the ground right around the base. A container is better, but stick to smaller varieties of bamboo, as larger ones will burst pots apart. Water and feed regularly to keep growth strong.

Strip lower leaves away each spring, and snip out skinny, weedy growth to make space for the thicker, more useful culms. You can cut these at any time of year: strip off the leaves, trim to length, and use green for plant supports or hang them horizontally in the shed for 2-3 months, to dry nice and evenly for long-term projects.

Bamboo's ramrod-straight stems make a living fence.

How to make a solitary bee hotel

You will need:
About 8m (25') of hollow bamboo
A 2-litre (4-US-pint) plastic drinks bottle
String

✳ Cut the bamboo up into equal lengths of about 15cm (6"). Then cut off the top of the drinks bottle, keeping the bottom 15cm of the bottle to make your bee hotel.

✳ Make a hole in the bottom of the bottle and thread string through, tying the ends together to make a loop.

✳ Now stuff the bottle tightly with bamboo, really jamming the stems in till you can't manage any more. Hang your bee hotel horizontally from the loop of string on a sunny, sheltered fence or wall, at about head height.

A slice of des-res heaven for a solitary bee.

Bees should start colonizing your hotel from the following spring, when they look for nesting sites. While they're around they should drop by your fruit blossom for a bit of pollinating too, paying you back with a bumper harvest.

Comfrey

Good for: Fertilizer, mulch, compost accelerator.

Most people walk right by my comfrey patch without even noticing, usually on their way to admire the giant cabbages next door. Yet that little cluster of plants is probably the most productive in the garden. Their lush, sand-papery leaves feed and mulch the asparagus and keep my tomatoes in fruit-laden good health. Any left over enriches the compost heap. Even the bees get the nectar-rich flowers: everyone's a winner.

Comfrey leaves are packed with goodness. In trials, comfrey came out higher in nitrogen, phosphorus and potassium than farmyard manure; it has more fruit-promoting potassium than commercial tomato feeds. Dilute that richness in water, and you pass it on to your plants.

Choose 'Bocking 14' comfrey, which flowers but is sterile, so doesn't self-seed itself rampantly like wild comfrey does. Half a dozen plants provide a steady supply of free fertilizer. I reserve pure liquid comfrey for fruiting plants – tomatoes in particular – but you can tweak home-made feeds to your own ends (see box on page 209).

Comfrey 'Bocking 14' doesn't set viable seed, so won't become a weed in your garden.

Growing and using

'Bocking 14' is propagated from root cuttings, so beg or buy some in to get your patch started. Plant about 60cm (2') apart in reasonably good soil, whether in sun or quite deep shade (this is an ideal crop for that awkward spot in the veg patch where nothing else will grow). Enclose the bed with an edging of wooden planks: though 'Bocking 14' doesn't self-seed, it will spread if you let it.

Give your comfrey patch a year to settle in, then start harvesting. Once the foliage gets to about 30cm (12") tall, shear it all back to about 15cm (6") above ground and collect to use as required. It re-grows rapidly after each cut, so expect three to four harvests each year.

Flavour your spuds

Comfrey is said to improve the flavour and yield of potatoes! Line the potato trench with comfrey leaves before planting, or simply apply it as a mulch to boost your crop.

How to make comfrey tea

You will need:
A good armful or two of comfrey leaves
A bucket with a lid
A brick
Water
An old sieve
Plastic milk cartons

❋ Cram the comfrey leaves into the bucket: the more you can get in, the richer your plant feed will be. Put the brick on top to hold them in place, then fill the bucket with water.

❋ Seal with the lid, as once it gets going comfrey tea stinks to high heaven and attracts flies from miles around. Leave in a distant corner for about 6 weeks to stew.

❋ Once it's done – it should be the colour of weak tea – pour through the sieve to filter out the debris, then bottle in clean plastic milk cartons. Comfrey tea keeps happily in the shed for several weeks.

Make your own fertilizers

It's not just comfrey: you can make liquid fertilizers from all sorts of other greenery in the garden. Anything you would normally put on the compost heap – and quite a lot you wouldn't – can be made into liquid fertilizer. (Compost tea is the perfect way to put your worst weeds to good use.)

While comfrey tea is just the thing for fruiting plants, nettle tea is particularly nitrogen-rich, so is perfect for growing youngsters and leafy greens. Mix both together for an all-purpose feed. Keep a bucket stewing at all times, and you need never buy fertilizer again.

Nettles: Rich in nitrogen, leafy green stinging nettles make a powerful booster for rapid leafy growth, so use the feed on any growing plant but especially salads, spinach and young plants. For the richest concentration of nutrients, shear the nettles off to the ground while they're still young and before they've flowered. Stew in a bucket in the same way as for comfrey tea.

Manure: The best ingredient for a general plant pick-me-up, horse manure takes 6 months to rot down in the compost heap but just 6 weeks when it's soaked in water to make manure tea. Fill an old pillowcase or some nylon tights with manure and dunk it into the bucket to soak, and dilute before using.

Ground elder and other weeds: Leafy weeds of any sort make good compost tea, including real nasties like ground elder, bindweed, docks and rampant annuals like hairy bittercress. Pull up or hoe off before they set seed or flower, and pack into a bucket to soak for an all-round fertilizer.

Perennial weed roots: You can't compost the white rope-like roots of bindweed, ground elder or couch grass, or they'll survive to regenerate next year. So drown them in water for a couple of months instead, and use the by-product to feed your plants. It's enough to make you believe in karma.

Young and nitrogen-rich nettles make the perfect liquid fertilizer for leafy crops.

New Zealand flax

Good for: String, netting, net bags, support wires, baskets.

You don't have to give up growing ornamental garden plants if you're growing your own food. Lots of garden plants are more than just pretty faces. Elaeagnus, for example, is a popular hedging shrub but also has snackable berries, as do fuchsias (see Chapter 4); indeed you can eat lilac flowers, daylily buds and hollyhock leaves too.

My favourite, though, is more useful than edible: the sturdy evergreen New Zealand flax (*Phormium tenax*), known in my garden as the string plant. That's because inside each wide, strappy leaf is a sheet of tough fibres stronger than any jute. Whenever I want to tie up tomatoes or train in an errant bean shoot, I reach for a piece of flax.

If you're being particular and want string that looks like string, scrape off the top layer of greenery to reveal the fibrous strands underneath, then twist a few together and plait. It's a job you can do in front of the telly, and home-made string netting looks ten times prettier than the green plastic variety.

But I rarely have time to watch telly, never mind plait string, so I take the short cut. Just slice off a leaf and split it with a thumbnail. It strips easily into colourful strands about 1m (3') long, ample for every job from tying in delicate little sweet-pea shoots to lashing together bean wigwams. Best of all, the plant is evergreen, perennial and long-lived – so you never run out.

The handsome New Zealand flax is also one of the most useful plants you can have in your garden.

Growing and using

Phormiums are tough as old boots: they think nothing of exposed coastal spots, and grow in sun or shade. They also cope well with the dry, restricted conditions in containers, and in damp gardens this may be a better option, as the one thing phormiums dislike is sitting in soggy soil. Remember to feed and water regularly in containers, though, as the roots quickly fill the space.

Phormiums do grow quite large in time – up to 2.4m (8') – but you can lift and divide them when they outstay their welcome, or take an offshoot from the main plant and start again.

How to make netting

You will need:

A good quantity of New Zealand flax leaves

Drawing pins

❋ Make several lengths of string by splitting the leaves into strands.

❋ Pin one length horizontally to a wall or fence: this will be the edge of your net.

❋ Fold the other lengths in half and hitch on to the horizontal string, to leave pairs of strands hanging down at intervals.

❋ Now start knotting. Take the first two strands and tie together with an overhand knot to make a triangle. Work along each row in turn like this, knotting alternate pairs of strands to make a net of diamond shapes.

❋ Finally, take another line the same length as the top and pin it along the bottom edge of your net. Then tie each strand individually on to it to finish.

To make the net finer or coarser, just adjust the spacing between the strands.

Tomatoes need tying in? Reach for a strand of flax.

Home-grown weedkiller

Grow your own living weedkiller by planting the enormous French marigold relative *Tagetes minuta* (Mexican marigold or southern marigold). It's around 1.8m (6') tall and not that great to look at, but the magic is in the roots: they give off toxic chemicals which inhibit the growth of any other plants nearby, including bindweed, couch grass and ground elder.

So, if you've got a particularly infested patch, clear out any plants you want to keep and plant this bruiser instead (raised from seed under cover in early spring). After a year or two of this you'll find that even the most persistent perennial weeds are on the run, for good. It's an annual, so as soon as you've cleared your weedy patch just remove the marigolds and plant up as usual the following spring.

Mexican marigolds: nature's own weedkiller.

Mix your own potting compost

If you're making your own garden compost – and if not, you should be (you'll find basic instructions in Chapter 6) – you have the raw ingredients for self-sufficiency in raising seedlings and container plants too.

Mixing your own potting compost isn't the dark art it's often made out to be. In fact, given the variable quality of a lot of bagged composts these days, you may well find that yours is an improvement on your usual brand. And, because the soil you use is the stuff that's already in your garden, your plants will have a head start from the first.

For most composts, you'll need just these few ingredients:

❋ well-rotted garden compost and soil, both sieved to remove debris
❋ a gritty component for drainage, such as sand or horticultural grit
❋ a low-nutrient base, such as leafmould, coir or composted bark.

Home-made compost gives youngsters a flying start.

Leafmould is the best (and most self-sufficient) base, but you can't buy it in the shops, so will need to make it yourself. Collect autumn leaves in a simple bin made of chicken wire stapled to four posts (failing this, you can use black bin bags with holes punched through them), and leave them to rot for at least a year; preferably two. After that it'll be a lovely, crumbly, sweet-smelling, black growing medium. While you're waiting for your leafmould to mature, you can buy in similarly low-nutrient, though less self-sufficient, substitutes like coir (coconut fibre) or composted bark.

You will need a wheelbarrow, spade and sieve, plus your ingredients. Then measure out your quantities, sieved as necessary, and start mixing. It's a bit like cooking, really, though you don't have to be too pernickety about measuring everything exactly: a pinch of this and a handful of that is the approach. Make a batch or two following the recipes below, grow some plants in it and keep notes – then you can adjust as required until you have just the mix that works for you.

Seed compost

A low-nutrient, finely sieved mix for starting off seeds; add a little extra sand and you can use it for rooting cuttings too. Note that home-made seed compost will contain lots of weed seeds, and occasionally soil-borne diseases which may affect your seedlings – so if you can, sterilize it in a microwave before use.

Most of the raw ingredients for home-made potting compost can be had for free.

❄ One part leafmould
❄ One part sand
❄ One part garden compost

Potting-on compost

A medium-nutrient mix for young plants: great for pricking out and potting-on seedlings.

❄ One part leafmould
❄ One part garden compost
❄ One part topsoil

Multipurpose compost

For potting-on young plants and growing fruit, veg or herbs in containers.

❄ One part leafmould
❄ One part sand
❄ Two parts garden compost
❄ Two parts topsoil

Keeping livestock brings a whole new level of joy into your self-sufficient life.

Chapter Thirteen
SUPPLY YOUR OWN EGGS AND MEAT

"Not all livestock demand much space or time for their care, and giving them a good life is its own reward."

The day the first chickens arrived at the end of my garden (a modest strip of suburbia that was also home to a Wendy house and trampoline), I felt like I'd somehow graduated. I'd started out dabbling with a few veg, and now here I was supplying my own eggs as well. It was entirely coincidental that I'd also acquired eight feathery pets which had names and followed me around in the hope of an earthworm. Now the breakfast scrambled eggs as well as the fried tomatoes were from our back garden. It was perhaps inevitable that I'd start wondering about the bacon too.

I now keep sheep, chickens and the occasional pig or two, and provide much of the meat we eat, yet I fit in my fledgling farm around full-time work plus teenage family life. Though I do have a large garden, I don't own any other land. Expanding your self-sufficiency capacity is possible even with quite limited resources, if you're determined enough.

And the first time you sit down to a roast where you know exactly how the animal it came from has been treated, from the moment it was born, is a point of no return. You've come full circle: every mouthful of food on that plate is there because you put it there – no secrets, no hidden ingredients, just as nature intended. It's honest meat eating: and my, does it taste good.

In this chapter you'll find profiles of the animals that fit in comfortably around a busy schedule and adapt well to life with a part-time farmer. It's beyond the scope of this book to give more than an outline of the care for each animal, so if you're keen to know more, sign up for a course or study day: they're now available for everything from beekeeping to pig care, lambing and poultry-keeping. Once you have the basics under your belt, you're ready to get your stock and get started on one of the most fulfilling and exhilarating self-sufficiency adventures there is. You'll never look back.

LIVESTOCK AND MODERN LIFE

It's surprising how well livestock-keeping fits in with a normal lifestyle. It takes about half an hour to visit my gaggle of animals each morning, just after I've seen the kids off to school and before I start work. An extra hour or two at weekends takes care of fencing, mucking out and routine care.

But it is a responsibility. Living creatures are entirely dependent on you for food, water and

Kids and livestock do mix – beautifully.

welfare. The livestock you'll read about in this chapter are those I've found to be most compatible with a busy lifestyle, and they are, on the whole, low-maintenance and undemanding. The approximate amounts of time given here for their care are the minimum: it's what you can get away with when everything is going well. If you have time, you'll probably want to linger a little anyway (sheep in particular love a scratch behind the ears).

But as with all dependants, there are occasional little crises when they need your attention for longer. Emergencies are rare if you take good day-to-day care of your animals, but sometimes you do have to drop everything at a moment's notice. And from time to time they need to be your first priority – I cut work to a minimum for the month when the sheep are lambing, for example. Flexible working helps, as does sharing the load – and produce – with a fellow self-sufficiency nut.

Animals without the land

Not only do you not have to become a small-holder to keep animals for food; neither do you need land of your own. A beehive fits on to a balcony. Many allotment sites let you keep chickens. For larger livestock, look for scraps of land of about a hectare (a couple of acres) – too small to interest farmers but large enough for a handful of sheep. Often the owners are delighted to have someone look after it, and charge little rent: I pay for one of my fields with an annual shoulder of lamb.

There's agricultural land to be found in the suburbs not far from the centre of quite major cities too, and urban nature reserves often include grazing land. I knew one lady who lived in a flat in central Cambridge and kept alpacas a few miles away, visiting them daily on her moped before work.

ANIMALS FOR PART-TIME FARMERS

All these animals fit in well around a busy twenty-first-century life, needing minimal land and relatively little maintenance. Start with a beehive in the back garden, and graduate to pigs or sheep for self-sufficiency in meat (and more) without the smallholding.

Bees

Land required: None – you can keep a beehive on a balcony.
Time required: 20 minutes per hive per week in summer, or fortnightly in winter; plus one day twice a year to take off the honey.

Starter breeds: There are several different strains of honeybee: source locally and try to find calmer strains, which will be easier to look after.
Produce: One hive produces plenty for a household – 9-18kg (20-40lb) of honey a year, plus honeycomb, beeswax and propolis, a brownish resin with antibiotic properties.

Beekeeping is within your reach wherever you live, as a beehive takes up so little room. You just have to look at the balconies and roof gardens of London to convince yourself that beekeeping is possible in very small spaces. In fact, there's evidence that bees in cities actually do better than bees in the countryside, as they get more nectar from the small, intensively gardened pockets of flowers in city gardens than from the huge barren monocultures of intensive agriculture.

Beekeeping is an immensely absorbing hobby.

> *Keeping bees helps to boost ailing bee populations – on which we are all dependent for crop pollination.*

A course in beekeeping is a must, to ensure you know the basics before you begin.

There are very good reasons for keeping bees, quite apart from getting yourself a hobby of Zen-like calm and absorption. If you do have a vegetable garden, they will help to max out your harvest – especially of blossoming fruit and beans. And the honey they produce allows you to become self-sufficient in sugar, which is otherwise impossible unless you live in the Caribbean or grow a lot of sugar beet. Honey is a good substitute for sugar in most recipes, and a lot better for you too. And by no means the least important reason is to help boost ailing honeybee populations – on which we are all very much dependent for pollinating our crops.

That's not to say that beekeeping is easy, and keeping your bees happy, productive and healthy can sometimes be quite a challenge. Even experienced beekeepers will tell you they're still learning – which is one of the reasons it's such an absorbing hobby. Start by joining your local beekeeping club (in the UK they're regulated by the British Beekeepers Association), which will point you in the right direction. A course in beekeeping is a must to make sure you know the basics before you begin, from day-to-day care to how to avoid potential disasters like varroa mite infestations. Your local association can also help you get hold of your first colony.

Check with your neighbours before you start to keep bees, as not everyone feels happy about having tens of thousands of potentially pain-inflicting insects coming and going over the garden fence every day. Try to be considerate about siting your hive: find an out-of-the-way place, away from dog walkers, children and livestock if possible. If it's on the ground, it's worth positioning it facing a high obstacle such as a hedge, which makes the bees fly up quickly, well over the heads of any nearby people.

Bees will bustle about their business of making your honey, demanding minimal attention in return.

early and late summer – a patient, methodical process of persuading the bees to the bottom of the hive while you remove the honeycomb and extract the honey to fill dozens of jars with glowing amber sweetness. There are few things in life which offer so much reward for so little effort.

Chickens

Land required: Each hen needs a minimum 0.3m² (4sq ft) in the coop, plus the same in the outside run: so a flock of four needs 2.4m² (26sq ft) of space in total. Larger breeds need more; bantams less.

Time required: 20 minutes twice a day (first thing in the morning and last thing at night), plus half an hour at weekends to muck out.

Good starter breeds: Welsummer, Light Sussex.

Produce: About five eggs per week per chicken (fewer in winter for non-battery hens); five or six hens will keep a family in eggs more or less year-round. Plus there's the option of meat – although this is one for more rural situations, as you'll require space for a lot of chickens, plus a cockerel, to make it worthwhile.

You'll start with a 'nucleus' or 'nuc' – a small colony of bees on brood frames, including a young laying queen plus a retinue of worker bees. Every beekeeper has a favourite hive: Langstroth are the traditional 'stack' style and produce the most honey, but top bar hives are easier for beginners – these are rather like wooden mangers with wooden bars across the top. The bees build their combs straight on to the bars, with no frames required. They're a lot lighter and easier to use, but you'll need to inspect them more often, as the bees can sometimes attach the combs to more than one bar.

Beekeeping is about as low-maintenance as livestock-keeping gets. Half an hour a week to check all is well, and that's it through summer – it's even less time-consuming in winter, when you only need to check them occasionally. The only real work comes when you're harvesting your honey, twice a year, in

Hens are delightful to have around the place, as they scratch away busily, crooning to themselves and rolling around ecstatically in dust baths. They're usually the first choice for back-garden livestock, as they need relatively little space and give so much in return.

Don't believe those who try to convince you that hens will be happy in a portable run. Even if you move it regularly they are likely to get bored: hens are naturally free-ranging animals

Hens are the ultimate in backyard self-sufficiency.

and get frustrated if they're too cooped up. If you only have room for a smaller run, keep bantams instead: they still lay (slightly smaller) eggs but are half the size, so more content in a restricted space.

A good-quality hen house or converted small garden shed with a perch and nest boxes is essential, as is as much access to outdoor space as possible. If you're around a lot during the day, you may be able to let your chickens range free throughout your garden. They can be quite destructive, though – they don't usually eat plants (with a few exceptions: they're very partial to chard and anything with berries), but they do scratch so enthusiastically that they often pull plants out by the roots.

The other difficulty with completely free-ranging chickens is Mr Fox. Especially in urban areas, foxes are fearless and will repeatedly visit a garden, day and night, till they've got the lot. The only real answer is to fence an area for your chickens so well that the fox can't get in. Chicken-wire fences about 2m (6'6") high, buried 30cm (1') into the ground at the bottom, work best. I make mine wobbly by putting in stakes to only half the height and then threading bamboo canes through the wire in the top half, so it's held upright but not rigid enough for a fox to climb over. A thread

Keep hens well protected against the fantastic (but rather bloodthirsty) Mr Fox.

of electrified wire about 30cm above ground, all the way around the run, stops him investigating too closely if he's thinking about tunnelling under.

Another constant issue when keeping hens is vermin. Where you have chickens, you have rats – the ultimate opportunists when it comes to stealing corn, layer's pellets and even eggs. Rat-proof feeders, which operate by the chicken standing on a spring-loaded plate to release the feed, help to keep numbers down; collecting eggs promptly helps too.

You'll need to visit your chickens twice a day: early in the morning to let them out, and last thing at night to put them to bed. Feed them layer's pellets ad lib via a hopper during the day. I also scatter a little mixed corn on the ground for them to scratch up in the afternoon. Once you're into the swing of it, all this becomes a delightful part of your daily routine – all the more so when you can bring home a handful of eggs still warm for your breakfast.

Pigs

Land required: About 10m x 10m (33' x 33') makes a generous pen for two weaners.
Time required: 20 minutes twice a day for feeding and checking, plus half an hour for cleaning out at the weekends.
Good starter breeds: Saddlebacks, Gloucestershire Old Spot.
Produce: Pork, bacon, ham and sausages in vast quantities – one pig keeps our family in porky products for a year.

I once spoke to a teacher at a school with a modest garden which kept pigs, cared for by the pupils, who learned a great deal along the way about food production, good husbandry and the business of selling produce to parents, staff and visitors. I was a little sceptical about all this: wouldn't the pigs smell, after all?

The secret, the teacher told me, was that they didn't keep the pigs over winter. Then, he explained, you avoid the smelly, muddy stage: pigs in summer are relatively clean animals, don't smell as much and are extremely useful rotovators. The pigs had one side of the garden and spent the summer happily rooting about, turning over and fertilizing the soil. Then off they went to the abattoir in autumn, and the following spring the patch where they had been was planted with potatoes, and another pair of pigs arrived to turn over the other side of the garden.

Raising weaners for slaughter isn't, strictly speaking, self-sufficiency, as you're buying in your stock from another pig producer each year. But it is the most practical way to keep pigs in a limited space. When you have to be considerate to your neighbours and you don't

Pigs are real characters and a delight to have around.

want to have to hold your nose every time you go into your garden, avoiding the time when pigs are at their most antisocial is just good sense. It's also better tailored to your needs when you're trying to produce only as much as you can eat. Keep a sow over winter and let her farrow, and she could produce over 20 piglets. When you only need one or at most two to keep you and your family fed, the trouble and effort of selling the rest is really more than a non-commercial producer needs.

Gilts – female pigs – are the most prized, as it is often claimed that the meat of a boar will

taste 'tainted'. However, pig-keeping friends tell me that as long as you keep male weaners away from sows, and slaughter them before they reach maturity at 6 months, you won't notice a difference. Male weaners are cheaper to buy too, and you won't feel tempted to keep them.

You'll need to keep more than one weaner, as pigs are very sociable, intelligent animals, and pine without company. They'll need a sturdy pig ark, about 2m x 2m (6'6" x 6'6") – these are traditionally made of corrugated iron, but you can use or build anything that's

Like rotovators on legs, pigs turn land over efficiently.

Keep more than one pig, as they need the company.

You'll need to keep more than one weaner, as pigs are very sociable and intelligent animals.

strong enough to cope with pigs rooting around inside. Line the house with a thick bed of straw, topped up occasionally through-out summer.

You'll also need a very well-fenced run: pigs are powerful creatures, and shove over half-hearted barriers without a second thought. Sink sturdy posts into the ground every 2-3m (6'6"-10') and fence with galvanized pig mesh,

then add two strands of electric fencing at about 30cm and 60cm (1' and 2') above ground, and connect to the mains (preferably) or a 25V leisure battery, kept well charged. They'll only touch it once or twice – with accompanying outraged squeals – before learning their lesson.

Once you have the accommodation sorted, though, pigs are straightforward to look after. A twice-daily feed of pig nuts keeps them happy, plus any surplus or past-their-best veg from the garden and other scraps (except meat). Start your pigs on sow and weaner pellets, and switch to fattening and finishing feed for the last couple of months. Be careful not to overfeed them, though: you're aiming at a slow, steady weight gain through the year for the best-quality meat.

Pigs are generally quite tidy creatures and will mess in one corner of the run: 10 minutes with the shovel and you've got clean pigs and a bucket of rich manure for the compost heap. They'll turn over the ground to bare soil quite quickly – pigs are a great way to clear waste ground. For a treat, tip a bucket or two of water on the ground in one corner to let them have a good wallow. Watch out for sunburn, and make sure your pigs can get out of the sun in hot spells. Otherwise, illness in a well-cared-for pig is rare.

Sheep

Land required: A hectare (about 2 acres) will support two to four ewes.

Time required: 20 minutes a day to check your flock, plus half a day every 6 weeks to deal with routine care such as feet trimming, shearing and spraying against flystrike. Once a year in spring, lambing requires your presence regularly – every few hours plus last thing at night and first thing in the morning when lambs are imminent – for about a month.

Good starter breeds: Southdown, Texel.

Produce: Lamb – two ram lambs feed our family for a year. Also hogget (meat from older lambs, said to have a richer flavour) and mutton. Wool – depending on the breed, you will get about 2.5kg (5lb 8oz) of raw fleece from each sheep per year.

My little flock of Dorset Down sheep started with two wary and flighty little ewe lambs bought from a flock in the next-door county and tipped into a rented field, blissfully unaware that they were about to be the guinea pigs in my new sheep-keeping experiment. Those lambs are now great-grandmas, grown big, placid and content, and the flock has grown to eight. It's been a heck of a ride.

Sheep have the ability to be frustrating and delightful, in more or less equal measures. I am still made to feel like a rank amateur at various stages of every year, as they develop some new ailment or complication. But just occasionally I feel like I might be beginning to know what I'm doing – and there's no deeper satisfaction than looking over the fence at your ewes, some of whom you watched being born, grazing with their own lambs in the summer sunshine.

On the whole, sheep are surprisingly little trouble. Mostly, it's just a daily check to make sure all is well. Once every 6 weeks or so I bring them into a pen of hurdles to trim feet and carry out other routine jobs like dagging (trimming the wool around their backsides so it doesn't get too foul and attract flies), spraying against flystrike or tagging the growing lambs. You don't need a sheepdog when your sheep are tame: they'll follow you pretty much anywhere, including into a trailer, for a bucket of sheep nuts and a scratch behind the ears.

About three or four times a year, though, my sheep get a little more labour-intensive. Autumn is a busy time, taking this year's ram lambs to the abattoir and then splitting the breeding ewes from the rest of the flock before getting in the ram. I rent my ram from a local sheep farmer for a couple of months, giving him plenty of time to tup (mate with) my ewes. I collect him in early winter for a mid-spring lambing – much better than lambing in late winter, as with commercial flocks, as it's warmer and there's fresh grass and

My first home-bred ewe, Pie, is now a mum herself.

Giving your stock a good death

When you're raising meat for your own consumption, with stock welfare a top priority, how you kill your animals is as important as how you look after them. For your own sake, it's a good idea not to name any animals you know you're going to eat: I try not to handle them too much either, and keep my distance. Forming a relationship with them just makes things harder.

While you can kill smaller animals like chickens at home (there are courses in humane slaughter available), you'll need to take larger animals like sheep and pigs to the abattoir. But rather than opting for the one used by local farmers, which is likely to handle extremely large numbers of animals, seek out smaller, family-run abattoirs. Ask your local smallholding group, as they will know all the local abattoirs by reputation.

Keep stress to a minimum by bringing your animals in to the trailer quietly and loading them with as little fuss as possible. For the same reason, try to find an abattoir that's as local as possible, so they don't face a long drive in the trailer.

Most abattoirs will also butcher your meat for you: this is an option well worth taking up, as doing it yourself is no small undertaking. You collect your animals ready-jointed and labelled in a large plastic bag which you can then decant into the freezer, ready to eat.

Congratulations – it's twins!

Sheep-keeping is undoubtedly a step closer to a smallholding lifestyle: for a start, you have to get your head around actually having your own animals killed. But it's within the reach of anyone with access to a little land. And there's a melt-in-the-mouth flavour to meat from grass-raised stock, bred above all for eating quality, with a tenderness that comes from low-food-miles, low-stress production.

more daylight. One of the huge advantages of keeping sheep on a very small scale is that your decisions are governed not by stock market prices but by whatever makes your (and your animals') life easier.

Lambing takes over my life for about a month or so in spring. I've learned the hard way that you must be well organized: stock up several weeks ahead on everything you'll need, from iodine to antibiotics and syringes from the vet. You will be treating your animals yourself in all but the direst of cases: I've become very used to my role as amateur vet, from injecting medication to easing a hand inside a ewe to straighten a twisted lamb.

Other animals

The animals described so far in this chapter are the easiest for a part-time smallholder to keep – but of course there are dozens more. Weigh up the pros and cons carefully and you could expand your menagerie even further.

Alpacas: Fantastic characters and exceptionally good wool – but no other products.

Cows: Delightful and highly productive, but a real smallholder's animal, as the commitment required is huge.

Ducks: Great slug and snail control and lots of fun. The eggs are delicious, but the birds are a little mucky.

Goats: Wonderful meat; delicious milk and cheese. They're real escape artists, so fence them well.

Rabbits: Lovely meat and lots of it. Fencing them in can be tricky, and foxes love them.

Goats are a good solution for self-sufficiency in milk if you can't keep cows.

Rules and regulations

You don't need to worry about registering backyard animals like poultry or bees, but for larger livestock, including sheep, pigs, cows and goats, even the tiniest flock must be registered with the local authorities. There's also a degree of paperwork involved in moving them, breeding and slaughtering.

In the UK, you must register your 'smallholding' (even if it's just rented land or your garden) and tag farm animals with your registration number, as well as sending back detailed annual flock returns and reports of any veterinary treatment given. Regulations are slightly different for each type of animal and vary from country to country, so do look into what's required before you start: your government agricultural department should be able to help set you up with what you need.

Resources

Growing your own fruit, veg and livestock is an absorbing preoccupation: 20 years after I started, I'm still learning more every day. There's a huge number of organizations, suppliers, books and websites out there waiting to help you further your own knowledge: here are just a few to get you started.

Organizations

You can achieve so much more when you have the support and reassurance of experts on tap. These organizations are mines of expertise on all things to do with growing your own food (for livestock, see page 231.)

American Horticultural Society (AHS)
Washington DC, USA
www.ahs.org
The AHS has been providing advice, help and guidance for gardeners in America for nearly a century. Their gardens at River Farm have an orchard, and they hold regular Master Gardener sessions on vegetable- and fruit-growing.

Garden Organic and the Heritage Seed Library
Coventry, UK
www.gardenorganic.org.uk
Garden Organic is a hub for gardeners who want to do it the natural way. Members of its Heritage Seed Library can access a unique collection of rarely grown heirloom veg seeds.

GIY Ireland
Waterford, Republic of Ireland
www.giyinternational.com
GIY (Grow It Yourself) Ireland provides invaluable help and encouragement for veg gardeners in over 80 active local groups in Ireland, plus another five in Australia.

The Herb Society
Liverpool, UK
www.herbsociety.org.uk
Founded in 1927, the Herb Society is still dispensing down-to-earth information, research, anecdotes and education about the many uses of culinary, medicinal and cosmetic herbs.

The Herb Society of America (HSA)
Kirtland, OH, USA
www.herbsociety.org
A huge resource for herb growers throughout the United States, with educational programmes and research into the uses of herbs. It also runs the National Herb Garden in Washington DC.

The National Allotment Society (NSALG)
Corby, UK
www.nsalg.org.uk
Campaigning for beleaguered allotment owners everywhere, NSALG is a mine of information about how to get your hands on and manage a plot.

The Royal Horticultural Society (RHS)
London, UK
www.rhs.org.uk
The RHS is a go-to resource for information and expertise on all things to do with growing. The fantastic website includes details of gardens across the country where you can see for yourself how the pros do it.

Royal New Zealand Institute of Horticulture (RNZIH)
Canterbury, New Zealand
www.rnzih.org.nz
A great resource of research and best practice, the RNZIH has provided advice, help and information to keen gardeners in New Zealand since the 1920s.

Société Nationale d'Horticulture de France
Paris, France
www.snhf.org
A highly respected horticultural organization, founded in 1827. Growing fruit and veg (as well as medicinal plants) is a big part of what they do.

La Via Campesina
Harare, Zimbabwe
https://viacampesina.org
'The International Peasant's Voice' is a worldwide

movement covering about 160 organizations in 73 countries, bringing together millions of small-scale farmers to defend sustainable agriculture.

WWOOF
International
www.wwoof.net
WWOOF stands for 'World Wide Opportunities on Organic Farms': it is an international movement linking volunteers with organic growers in countries around the world for hands-on experience of growing crops and raising animals for food.

Seed and plant suppliers

My favourite stockists are like old friends: I go back to them again and again to expand the range of veg I grow, replace varieties I've lost, and add to my knowledge by tapping into years of expertise.

Baker Creek Heirloom Seeds
Mansfield, MO, USA
www.rareseeds.com
America's leading vegetable seed supply specialist, Baker Creek majors in tried-and-tested heirloom varieties, all open-pollinated, so you can save your own seed.

The Diggers Club
Dromana, VIC, Australia
www.diggers.com.au
This hugely popular membership organization and seed merchant majors on heritage and organic vegetable seeds. You can see many of the varieties growing at Diggers' renowned open garden, Herons-wood, on the Mornington Peninsula.

Franchi Seeds of Italy
Milan, Italy
www.franchisementi.it; www.seedsofitaly.com
An old and much-respected Italian seed company, with branches all over Europe. They have an interesting range of veg varieties and really generous packets of seed.

Graines Baumaux
Nancy, France
www.graines-baumaux.fr
One of the larger veg seed companies in France, with a mouthwatering selection of tomatoes, kales, chicories . . . you name it, they've got it.

Jekka's Herb Farm
Bristol, UK
www.jekkasherbfarm.com
An outstanding selection of herb seeds and plants from the Queen of Herbs, Jekka McVicar. Also offers courses in herb garden design, propagation and using herbs.

Johnny's Selected Seeds
Fairfield, ME, USA
www.johnnyseeds.com
Johnny's is something of an institution in the States, with thousands of varieties, many bred on-site. The website is packed with useful tools, including a seed calculator and grower's library.

Livingseeds
Henley-on-Klip, nr Johannesburg, South Africa
http://livingseeds.co.za
A huge range of over 400 varieties of open-pollinated veg seeds for South African gardeners, including many heirloom varieties, with over 90 per cent of the seed raised on-site.

Pennard Plants
East Pennard, Somerset, UK
www.pennardplants.com
A good range of young plants and seeds, with an emphasis on heritage and unusual varieties. Includes a fabulous array of heirloom seed potatoes, which you can buy at Pennard's regular Potato Fairs.

The Real Seed Catalogue
Newport, Pembrokeshire, UK
www.realseeds.co.uk
Offers a very good range of open-pollinated vegetable seed, chosen so you can save the seed yourself – there are detailed instructions on the website.

Fruit- and orchard-tree suppliers

Choose your trees and soft fruit with particular care, as they'll be with you for years to come.

Adams County Nursery
Aspers, PA, USA
www.acnursery.com
Fruit tree specialists who supply stock to most of the commercial nurseries in the United States. A mouth-watering range of apples, peaches, cherries and nectarines – and lots more besides.

Agroforestry Research Trust
Totnes, Devon, UK
www.agroforestry.co.uk
An excellent place to buy fruit and nut trees, with some really unusual varieties. Very informative website; also offers courses in forest gardening and growing nuts.

Blackmoor Nurseries
Blackmoor, Hampshire, UK
www.blackmoor.co.uk
A very good range of fruit trees, soft fruit and strawberries at reasonable prices, with useful information on pollination groups and rootstocks.

Chris Bowers & Sons
Wimbotsham, Norfolk, UK
www.chrisbowers.co.uk
In the business for over 30 years, Chris Bowers has an exceptional range of soft fruit and fruit trees on a variety of rootstocks, including pre-trained trees and nuts.

Fruttidoro
Faenza, nr Bologna, Italy
www.fruttidoro.com
Fruit specialist with a long history stretching back to 1895. Now offers a good range of 'ancient or forgotten fruit trees', including several Italian heirlooms.

Ken Muir
Clacton-on-Sea, Essex, UK
www.kenmuir.co.uk
Multiple gold medal winner at the RHS Chelsea Flower Show and best known for an astonishing range of strawberries, Ken Muir is also good for other soft fruit, including raspberries and grapevines.

Lubera
Bad Zwischenahn, nr Oldenburg, Germany
www.lubera.com
An outstanding fruit tree breeder, supplying trees throughout Europe and the UK. Constantly innovating with new products.

Stark Bro's
Louisiana, MO, USA
www.starkbros.com
Selling fruit trees to American gardeners for over 200 years and still going strong, Stark Bro's is really gardener-friendly, with lots of handy fruit-growing gear and trees for small gardens.

Thunder Mountain Orchard & Nursery
Whangarei, New Zealand
www.thundermountain.net.nz
A small-scale operation producing heritage fruit trees adapted to growing in warmer climates, including apples, pears and plums, grown organically and grafted on-site.

Yalca Fruit Trees
Nathalia, Victoria, Australia
www.yalcafruittrees.com.au
Supplies most of Australia with heritage and modern varieties of fruit trees, including trees for small spaces and lots of intriguingly unusual varieties.

Preserving equipment suppliers

You do need a certain amount of kit before you start stocking up your home-grown drinks cabinet or preserves larder. These brands and suppliers have stood the test of time.

All Seasons Homestead Helpers
Poultney, VT, USA
www.homesteadhelpers.com
Provider of really useful all-purpose supplies for self-sufficiency: everything from apple presses to driers and canning products, plus garden supplies.

Ball and Kerr Canning
Fishers, IN, USA
www.freshpreserving.com
For high-quality jars and canning equipment with the trademarked Ball & Kerr lids, plus drinks-making equipment. The website is encyclopedic, with tips, troubleshooting and recipes.

Fowlers Vacola
North Melbourne, VIC, Australia
http://fowlersvacola.com.au
The best-known home-canning supplier in Australia, founded in 1915, with its own jar design using smooth necks and a three-piece lid system.

Kilner
Liverpool, UK
www.kilnerjar.co.uk
A long-established company dating back to 1840, and the last word in sturdiness and reliability for bottles, jars, maslin pans and other preserving equipment.

Le Parfait
Villeurbanne, France
www.leparfait.fr; www.leparfait.com
A legend in French preserving circles, Le Parfait has

been providing elegant jars, bottles and other equipment for well over a century. The website (in French and English) also features dozens of recipes.

Vigo Presses
Dunkeswell, Devon, UK
www.vigopresses.co.uk
Sturdy, well-made presses for apples and other fruit, including those small enough for home use. Also sells cider-making equipment and fruit-picking gear.

Weck
Crystal Lake, IL, USA
www.weckjars.com
The characteristic strawberry logo is known across Germany and beyond as the mark of this long-established canning company, founded in Oflingen and now based in the USA. Jars feature glass lids, wide necks and rubber seals.

Livestock equipment and courses

When you're starting out, give yourself the best grounding you can. These organizations and resources offer help for beginners – from equipment and supplies to hands-on stock-keeping courses.

Alliance Elevage
Montmorillion, nr Poitiers, France
www.alliance-elevage.com
Everything the small-scale smallholder could want, from housing to feed to fencing. Ships right across Europe and beyond.

American Beekeeping Federation (ABF)
Atlanta, GA, USA
www.abfnet.org
National organization with over 4,700 members, bringing together beekeepers whether large- or small-scale around the country, with conferences, courses and campaigns.

Animal Arks
Callington, Cornwall, UK
www.animalarks.co.uk
Good, sturdy housing, including customized buildings, for animals small and large.

Backyard Poultry
Online-only
www.backyardpoultry.com
Lively Australian website linking small-scale poultry keepers right across Australia and New Zealand. Includes sales and wanted boards and an online shop.

The British Beekeepers Association
Kenilworth, Warwickshire, UK
www.bbka.org.uk
The umbrella group for beekeeping organizations around the country, many of whom offer beginners' courses in beekeeping.

Flyte so Fancy
Pulham, nr Dorchester, Dorset, UK
www.flytesofancy.co.uk
Hen houses, movable coops, broody coops, egg boxes, electrified poultry netting . . . if it's for chickens, it's here.

Homesteader's Supply
Sparta, TN, USA
www.homesteadersupply.com
All you could possibly want for self-sufficient living, with a huge range of smallholding supplies – from poultry products to milking equipment. Keep browsing and you'll find preserving equipment too.

Humble By Nature
Penallt, nr Monmouth, UK
www.humblebynature.com
Rural skills and smallholding school in rural Wales, owned by TV presenter Kate Humble. Offers dozens of courses, from general smallholding to lambing and butchery.

SustainLife
Near Waco, TX, USA
www.sustainlife.org
This homesteading school offers a huge curriculum, from beekeeping to cheesemaking, all run from a 1.5-hectare (4-acre) homestead in Texas. One-day, multi-day and online courses available.

Community gardening and CSAs

Finding a good community garden takes networking and a little research. These umbrella organizations can put you in touch with CSAs and community or shared garden schemes.

American Community Gardening Association (ACGA)
College Park, GA, USA
https://communitygarden.org
Brings together volunteers and supporters of community gardening organizations across the United States and Canada. The website includes a 'Find a Garden' tab.

CSA Network UK
UK-wide
https://communitysupportedagriculture.org.uk
Links Community Supported Agriculture organiza-
tions across the UK. The website can help you find
your nearest CSA and also lists events, networking
opportunities and resources.

European Federation of Allotments and Leisure Gardens
Luxembourg
www.jardins-familiaux.org
Continent-wide umbrella organization for allotment
gardens and gardeners, with a comprehensive list of
national allotment societies for each country.

European Federation of City Farms (EFCF)
Belgium
www.cityfarms.org
Brings together all shapes and sizes of city farm
across six countries in Europe (several more are
associate members). The website is a good resource
for tips and includes features on city-farm life.

Federation of City Farms and Community Gardens (FCFCG)
Bristol, UK
www.farmgarden.org.uk
A long-established umbrella network covering all
kinds of community gardening organizations, from
city farms to rural community gardens.

Green Guerillas
New York, USA
www.greenguerillas.org
This well-known urban greening pressure group and
networking organization promotes community
gardens and food-growing across America.

LocalHarvest
Santa Cruz, CA, USA
www.localharvest.org
A lively network linking CSA schemes right across
America. The website includes an online store
selling CSA farm produce, plus advice on joining
CSA schemes and a 'Find a CSA' button.

Prêter son Jardin
Montpellier, France
www.pretersonjardin.com
Online matching service linking garden owners
without the time to garden with would-be gardeners
with no land. Operates right across France via an
online forum.

Shared Earth
Austin, TX, USA
http://sharedearth.com
Perhaps the best-known garden sharing resource in
America, matching garden owners and wannabe
gardeners from DC to California and all points
between.

Urgenci
Aubagne, France
www.urgenci.net
An international network for CSA schemes, combin-
ing campaigning and research with information
about CSA schemes in Africa, Asia and Latin
America as well as the USA and Europe.

Good books

You can tell which reference books I rely on most
heavily: they're the ones whose spines are cracked
with use; the pages thumbed and muddy. This list
includes books I come back to time after time to
remind me of recipes, planting distances or the
many and varied diseases of sheep.

The Art of Fermentation: An In-depth Exploration
of Essential Concepts and Processes from
Around the World, Sandor Ellix Katz
(Chelsea Green Publishing Co, 2012)
A fascinating romp through every possible aspect of
fermentation, from sauerkraut and kimchi to yoghurt,
drawing on fermentation techniques from around
the world.

Back Garden Seed Saving: Keeping Our Vegetable
Heritage Alive, Sue Stickland
(Eco-Logic Books, 2008)
Now the must-have reference book for anyone
serious about saving their own seed from veg in the
back garden.

Backyard Self Sufficiency, Jackie French
(Aird Books Pty. Ltd, 2nd edn 2009)
An Australian classic and a very practical guide to
home self-sufficiency – covering a range of topics
from small animals to growing in difficult climates.

Ball Blue Guide to Preserving, various
(Alltrista Consumer Products, 2004)
A useful, practical guide to home canning, from the
leading US jar specialists. Includes detailed instruc-
tions on the various methods, plus timings and
recipes.

Easy Jams, Chutneys and Preserves, Val and John Harrison
(Right Way, 2009)
Down-to-earth and straightforward recipes for all my favourite jams and chutneys.

The Encyclopedia of Country Living, Carla Emery
(Sasquatch Books, 40th anniversary edn 2012)
An essential reference work, still in print and continuously updated 40 years after it was written, this is described as the "next best thing to having a live-in grandmother".

The Fruit Tree Handbook, Ben Pike
(Green Books, 2011)
Aimed at all levels of skill, from amateur to expert, this practical guide tells you all you need to know to grow fruit – from designing your orchard and planting your trees to harvesting your produce.

Grow Your Own Vegetables, Joy Larkcom
(Frances Lincoln, rev edn 2002)
If you buy only one vegetable-growing book, make it this one. Practical; to the point; authoritatively written by a veg-growing legend. You'll find absolutely everything you need to know within its pages.

Living on One Acre or Less: How to Produce All the Fruit, Vegetables, Meat, Fish and Eggs Your Family Needs, Sally Morgan
(Green Books, 2016)
An inspirational guide for the land-strapped livestock keeper and gardener, with lots of practical information and tips for producing food from a limited space.

The Self-Reliant Homestead: A Book of Country Skills, Charles A. Sanders
(Burford Books, 2003)
Hands-on, detailed advice on all aspects of self-reliant living, from choosing your land to raising livestock; making wines to making fences.

Good websites and online resources

Sometimes you need a quick answer and just have to ask someone. The following websites have the liveliest forums, reams of useful and authoritative features and dozens of tips and techniques at the click of a search engine.

www.accidentalsmallholder.net
Smallholding courses, recipes and some really informative articles – but best of all is the forum, where regulars include experienced shepherds and pig and poultry keepers, as well as gardeners.

www.backwoodshome.com
A Pacific coast website to accompany the magazine of the same name, with a lively forum and thought-provoking articles about every aspect of country living and homesteading.

www.countryfarm-lifestyles.com
Australian writer Malene Thyssen has collected her experiences of self-sufficient living in suburban Australia and in her 6-hectare (15-acre) farm in Italy, with topics from organic gardening to urban homesteading, crafts and livestock-keeping.

www.growfruitandveg.co.uk
The website of Grow Your Own magazine, with lots of good growing articles and a very lively forum, the Grapevine, where you can air (and usually solve) the thorniest of gardening problems.

www.herbnet.com
This absolutely encyclopedic American website includes exhaustive details of the habits and uses of every herb you can think of (and quite a few you can't).

www.motherearthnews.com
Among the first and still one of the most popular homesteading and sustainable lifestyle websites, this site runs alongside a paper magazine of the same name.

http://rediscover.co.nz
An endlessly interesting blog from New Zealand urban homesteader Julie Crean, with thoughtful posts on the challenges of self-reliance in a suburban bungalow.

www.selfsufficientish.com
Full of thought-provoking and informative articles on everything and anything you can grow or make for yourself at home, by folk trying to live more self-sufficiently whatever their resources.

http://urbanhomestead.org
The tale of the Dervaes family's experiments in self-sufficiency at their ordinary suburban house in Pasadena, just 15 minutes' drive from downtown Los Angeles. An inspirational lesson in how much you can achieve with limited resources.

Index

ALSO BY GREEN BOOKS

The Fruit Tree Handbook
"A must for anyone considering anything from a couple of trees to an orchard."
Mark Diacono, River Cottage Head Gardener

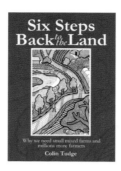

Six Steps Back to the Land
"Anyone who eats food should read this book."
***Home Farmer* magazine**

Organic Gardening
"One of the all-time great gardening books."
Mike Mason, Good Gardeners' Association

Creating a Forest Garden
"A seminal piece of work on sustainable gardening, written with great spirit and soul."
Alys Fowler, TV presenter and writer

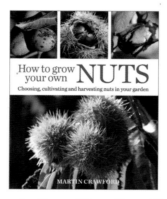

How to Grow Your Own Nuts
"The best guide I've seen to home and small-farm nut growing."
Eric Toensmeier, permaculturist and Yale University lecturer

An Orchard Odyssey
"Combines a dream of yore with a challenge for the future. Count me in."
Roy Lancaster, broadcaster and gardener

About Green Books

green books

Environmental publishers for 25 years.
For our full range of titles and to order direct from our website, see **www.greenbooks.co.uk**

Join our mailing list for new titles, special offers, reviews, author appearances and events:
www.greenbooks.co.uk/subscribe

For bulk orders (50+ copies) we offer discount terms. Contact **sales@greenbooks.co.uk** for details.

Send us a book proposal on eco-building, science, gardening, etc.: see **www.greenbooks.co.uk/for-authors**

 @ Green_Books   /GreenBooks